Raised Up!

Resurrection Testimonies

Julia Stevens

malcolm down
PUBLISHING

First published 2023 by Malcolm Down Publishing Ltd.
www.malcolmdown.co.uk

27 26 25 24 23   7 6 5 4 3 2 1

British Library Cataloguing in Publication Data
A catalogue record for this book is available from the British Library.

ISBN 978-1-915046-74-1

Unless otherwise indicated, Scripture quotations taken from the
One New Man Bible, copyright © 2011 William J. Morford.
Used by permission of True Potential Publishing, Inc.

Cover design by Angela Selfe
Art direction by Sarah Grace

Printed in the UK

Endorsements

He is the same Holy Spirit. He is the same Lord of Lords. What happened in the Bible still happens today. And that is the reason of this book. It's challenging and reflective at the same time. Read it and allow the Holy Spirit to challenge you in your own walk with God. May every one of us have the privilege of seeing the miracles of God outworked in our own lives. May we see the resurrection life of Christ reflected in us as we seek to bring that life to those around us. And, Julia, thank you for the encouragement!

Ralph Turner
Writer and Biographer

I thoroughly recommend this faith-filled, timely book written by Julia Stevens, one of my closest friends from childhood, a real woman of faith and integrity. This exciting book will encourage you to step out and believe God for the impossible. In the more than thirty years I have spent on the mission field, as I've taken God at His word and stepped out, I've seen God doing extraordinary things, including seeing Him raise people from the dead.

Having worked on the mission field alongside some of the people whose testimonies are in this book, I can verify the authenticity of their accounts. In fact, when serving on the Harvest School in Mozambique in 2010,

I spent time with an indigenous pastor who'd recently been raised from the dead through the prayers of Heidi and Rolland Baker and team, one of the fifty-three mentioned in the CBN media article.

As you read the awesome testimonies in this book, may you be encouraged to step out and see God doing mighty miracles through you too. It's what you were created for. Don't settle for anything less.

Paula O'Keefe
Missionary, and author of Miracles in the Midst of War

It is refreshing to see a book talking about resurrection of the dead. This was a primary teaching and doctrine of the early church and one that seems to have been left on the shelf these days. With lots of talk of the rapture and little if any teaching on the resurrection of the dead, it is refreshing to see Julia Stevens taking the bull by the horns and coming back to the importance of this teaching.

Having been raised from the dead myself, not once but twice, I am more than aware of what the Apostle Paul states in Romans 8 to be true. 'That same Spirit that rose Jesus from the dead is at work in our mortal bodies.' Resurrection from the dead is not just something that sometimes happens to a few Christians, it is our future hope and destiny that when Jesus returns we shall arise from the dead, immortal, to rule and reign as a kingdom of priests.

This book will give many fresh insight, joy and a blessed hope of what can happen this side of eternity, but what's also coming for all believers in Christ the other side of eternity.

Christopher Wickland
Senior Pastor, Living Word Church Network

Contents

1

Introduction

At the heart of the Christian faith and walk is resurrection from the dead and the spiritual 'resurrected life' in Jesus our Messiah. The apostle Paul writes in 1 Corinthians 15 that our faith is 'worthless' (v. 17, NASB) without resurrection because otherwise Jesus could not have risen from the dead and therefore, he could not make atonement for our many sins. Surrendering our lives to Messiah Jesus is of central importance to our faith, so that we 'may know Him and power of His resurrection, and the fellowship of His sufferings' (Philippians 3:10, NKJV).

Resurrection after life on this earth and into our heavenly bodies is our great hope. Our Lord Jesus died and rose again and was seen by more than 500 people[1] as well as His close friends the disciples. He left us His Holy Spirit so that we are enabled to live a righteous life 'raised up' in Him.

The word 'resurrection' in Greek, 'anastasis' and 'anistemi',[2] mean to 'rise up' and has roots in the words 'to raise up from lying down'.[3] In the written word of God there is a movement, an active life. During writing the beautiful

---

1. 1 Corinthians 15:6.
2. Strongs #G386, www.blueletterbible.org/lexicon/g386/nasb20/mgnt/0-1/ (accessed 29.1.24).
3. Strongs #G450 – anistēmi – Strong's Greek Lexicon (KJV), www.blueletterbible. org/lexicon/g450/kjv/tr/0-1/ (accessed 29.1.24).

words of this book I saw the image of a stunning Bride, the Bride to be of the Lamb. She was arising from sleep: 'Arise, shine; for your light has come, And the glory of the LORD has risen upon you' (Isaiah 60:1, NASB). The Bride in all her glory; raised up and raising up those who had 'fallen asleep' (John 11:11).

This book shares some of the keys of the kingdom of our Lord Jesus Christ and the how raising of the dead has happened in recent times and times past, not only in the incredible Word of God but also in ordinary people's lives as well as those who are full-time ministers of God. Our Lord chooses to work in different people's lives in many different ways, and this book includes testimonies with medical intervention and, miraculously, without.

Some Western testimonies include medical intervention, due to the fact that we have had a good medical support system generally in the West. In the developing world, the medical support system is not so much in evidence, and therefore people have a need to rely on natural remedies and spiritual means, in order to live and to thrive.

Eyewitness testimony both written and verbal have been used to verify facts in many spheres of study, including the fields of anthropology and sociology historical endeavour and journalism to name a few. I would put it to you, therefore, that trustworthy accounts of people who have seen resurrection occurring before their own eyes, especially those with many witnesses, should be taken seriously. If we do not accept eyewitness accounts, we are dismissing entire fields of knowledge.

Reports of resurrection of the dead appear throughout much of Church history. In the late second century, Irenaeus, an early Church father of the faith, noted an Orthodox Church in France where raisings from the dead were frequent. Resurrections were also among the documented miracles Augustine surveyed in Book 22 of *The City of God*.[4] John Wesley[5] also offered a first-hand account of a dead man being revived through prayer, recorded on the day it occurred, 25 December 1742.

Dr Craig Keener, a professor from Asbury University in Wilmore, Kentucky, USA, where there has been a recent revival, which began during penning these words, gives us guidance that: early twentieth-century testimonies are near impossible to verify today, however on occasion evidence remains. For instance, in 1907, a year after the Pentecostal Azusa Street Revival began, a revival newspaper called: *The Apostolic Faith*, testified that the raising of a Eula Wilson, whose blindness was also healed in the process of being raised from the dead.[6]

In his article 'Real Raisings from the Dead or Fake News?' Dr Keener writes that testimony and witness to resurrection are important in themselves to our faith. Dr Keener points out that if Jesus asked a leper to follow the instruction of scriptural 'prescription' to 'verify' his healing with a priest[7] it would be appropriate for us to verify miracles where it is possible. I have endeavoured to include those testimonies which are verified but where verification is not possible eyewitness account with witnesses are presented.

With regards to the testimonies in this book, I have spoken personally to most of the people either first or second-hand and can verify the trustworthiness of most

4. St Augustine, *The City of God, trans. William Babcock (New York*: New City Press, 2014).
5. Dr Craig Keener, 'Real Raisings from the Dead or Fake News?' Christianity Today, 17 May 2019, www.christianitytoday.com/ct/2019/june/miracles-resurrections-real-raisings-fake-news-keener-afric.html (accessed 30.1.24).
6. Keener, 'Real Raisings from the Dead or Fake News?' (accessed 30.1.24) and Craig S. Keener, *Miracles Today* (Ada, MI: Baker Academic, 2021).
7. Mark 1:44.

of the sources within these pages. Of course, I cannot say whether some of the quotes given may have been embellished or exaggerated; but these are the details as given to me. In the Bible there are accounts of resurrection which take place without verification but with witnesses; this is the biblical pattern which I follow. Where verification is available, it is mentioned. I hope the testimonies will impress at least those more open to faith and encourage a stronger belief that resurrection still happens today, and more than we would think.

Short teaching and current day testimony of accounts of those who have seen the dead rise back to life in the name of Jesus our Messiah make up *Raised Up!* I have written accounts of testimony from interviews, direct teaching or been given first-hand accounts of resurrection testimonies in peoples own words. Some testimonies also come from book excerpts; from research or people I am directly linked with. I hope these testimonies inspire your faith. *Raised Up!* has been written for the encouragement of hearts, and to build up faith, in the hope that many will gain more confidence to follow the upward call of all that Christ Jesus has for them to do and be.

There are millions of people throughout the world in different nations who claim to have witnessed great miracles of divine intervention;[8] these have even been surveyed. For example, in 2006 a survey was undertaken by Pew Research Center covering ten countries.[9]

According to Lee Strobel's book *The Case for Miracles*,[10] close to 100 million Americans believe in divine miracles.

---

8. 'Spirit and Power: A 10-Country Survey of Pentecostals', www.pewresearch. org/religion/2006/10/05/spirit-and-power/ (accessed 15.1.24).
9. Keener, 'Real Raisings from the Dead or Fake News?'.
10. Lee Strobel, *The Case for Miracles* (Grand Rapids, MI: Zondervan, 2018).

Indeed, worldwide there is a huge pool of believers in the miraculous who also believe in raising the dead.

One of the more personal reasons for writing this book is that when I was young, unbeknown to me, I witnessed someone dying in front of me. A lovely lady was introduced to me as newly joining the company where I then worked. During her first week of work. I was assigned to teach her the computer system. I got to know her a little better than some of my workmates. One day she dropped suddenly to the floor beside her desk. A few colleagues gathered around her. There were a few desks blocking the way between myself and her, and she was the other side of the room. I heard the Holy Spirit say to me: 'Go! Pray for her!' Instead, I simply froze and at that time, being a shy, self-conscious type, I thought: 'They are all attending to her, it would look strange for me to pray for her.' I did pray where I was, but I knew I had not obeyed the voice of the Lord adequately. I was more concerned about how I would look in other people's eyes, than for the lady's plight. Later on, that day she died; perhaps if I had obeyed God, she may have enjoyed more years with her loved ones on earth? I know I am forgiven, I have repented and have forgiven myself; but because of this, I have conviction and will now obey the Lord if ever a similar situation arises. In context I had witnessed a lady's ear being healed a few weeks beforehand and so had faith for miracles; it was the fear of man which caught me off guard, and perhaps a lack of faith.

Resurrection from the dead and the resurrected lifestyle is a huge subject which one of my mentors, Molly Sutherland of Resurrected Life Ministries,[11] was unable to cover fully, even though she held teachings numerous

---

11.   https://resurrectedlife.org/about.php (accessed 15.1.24).

times a week, every week for most of her later life. Similarly, in this book we have not covered every facet of this huge subject, which perhaps will take all of eternity to realise! However, I can say that it is a series of inspired nuggets for you to treasure.

I have always had a passion for reading – especially the Bible in its many translations, and mainly books of Christian non-fiction in the past few decades of my life. This reading has included the early church Fathers, the Apocryphal manuscripts, and reading Torah with Messianic Jewish teachers. I use these ancient historical manuscripts and background knowledge to show different perspectives of the day, knowing that they are not from the main inspired-of-God canon of Scripture, but that they are trusted people who wrote nearer the time of Jesus' death and resurrection. I may draw from these sources in helping to explore the inspiring subject of resurrection of the dead. This book is more about the reality of resurrection. There is some theology, teaching and observations included in most chapters. At the end of each chapter, there is an emphasis on testimony.

I hope you find joy and great encouragement as you read true testimony from those who watched a miracle happen before their very eyes: the dead come back to life. Our Lord is raising up His Holy Church in these darkening days.

2

What Does God Teach Us About Resurrection?

———◆———

You must wake up, sleeper,
and get up from the dead...
and the Messiah will shine upon you.

(Ephesians 5:14)

Every morning, we 'rise up'; it is the dawn of a brand-new day. One thing I have learned to do is to be grateful at the beginning of each day, which helps me walk into it with a focus on all that is good, all that is God. God's mercy is 'new every morning' and great is His faithfulness (Lamentations 3:23, NKJV).

Each day has the potential for flourishing life to spring up within us; Holy Spirit resurrection life. We can trust in the words, teaching and instructions of God for ourselves in the day ahead; to have simple faith like a child, walking with our Father God. We can dwell on *His* words for us, His love for us and our identity in Him. By the covering blood of Jesus, we are seen as holy and clean by our Father God as we turn away from worldly ways and look to His Way, Truth and Life.[12] We can lean into and learn from Him and

———

12. See John 14:6.

be aware of the holy presence of Holy Spirit; His present reality. We can ask Him about His thoughts for the day ahead, for a scripture, or about the help we may need. We can listen and learn, living a life given over to God, the one who is 'the Resurrection and the Life' (John 11:25). We can let Him know our thoughts, desires and issues. It's an everyday walk with our Lord God. Every day the Holy Spirit gives me a scripture and sometimes a song these often have meaning for the day or week ahead, or simply keep my Spirit flowing in His. Last week, for example, I woke to an old song, which the Lord reminded me:

Like dew in the morning your Spirit refreshes my soul,
And like honey on my lips your name is sweetness to me,
As I wait on you Lord my strength is renewed,
I rise up on eagle's wings.
To be in your presence,
To gaze on your face,
To sit at your footstool,
Here I find peace,
I set my eyes, only on you,
Beautiful Jesus,
I worship You.

The context was that I had been extraordinarily busy due to a heavy workload and very difficult circumstances. The song bought me into a continual place of peace which was much needed.

The focus of 'resurrection' is about our loving relationship with Jesus, our Lord of love. Our Loving Messiah has risen again from His sacrificial death into a ruling and reigning eternal life; our resurrected High Priest and King. He has taught us by example through His life of love and death, resurrection and ascension. Jesus left us His Holy Spirit on the earth before He rose to the right hand of our Father God, where He rules and reigns; we have His Spirit of resurrection life living within us; the very breath and resurrection life of Father God.

Resurrection life can be about the here and now present reality of our lives. We can be focused on His eternal glorious, loving resurrected life within us. Be aware that we are Father God's creation, His sons and daughters and His Spirit lives in us; our Father is continually speaking, but are we listening by faith? Jesus died and rose again so that we can also commune with our Father God. I have learned from the prayer of Jesus when He raised Lazarus from the dead that when He spoke to His Father God, He spoke with faith that our Father heard and would act on His words: 'Father, I give You thanks because You heard me' (John 11:41). Let us commune with faith in our hearts and in our words.

To be raised up, we have to die to our own ways, taking up our cross and surrendering our own will each day, to allow Father God's will to be done and His ways to happen in our lives. It is a daily walk and a developing process to be led by His Spirit, whose fruit is love, joy and peace, as we read in Galatians 5:22-23. Be led by His Spirit.

We can ask for 'His will be done', so that His kingdom comes, in us on earth, as it is in his heavenly realms.[13] It is only in the dying to our own will and ways, that His resurrection life can freely spring up. This is achieved in a myriad of small actions devotedly given and done to God. When you wake up, endeavour to read His Words from the Bible, listen to His voice and journal His words for you;

---

13. See Matthew 6:10.

communing with Him throughout the day and being aware of His presence is a key.

One small example of a life of practising the presence of God, is found in the testimony at the end of this chapter, my father left his own meal in order to help another who was in pain; forgetting his own desires to love his neighbour. There are many small examples in our action and interaction each day where we can lay down our lives in a righteous, vibrant way. These actions cause God's lovingkindness to flourish. Little by little, our lives are transformed by the words of the Lord and by His Spirit.

Obedience and a simple surrendered loving life to the Lord God of the dynamic Holy Bible, from a place of relationship, love and intimacy, are the main keys to resurrection. It is not a weak life of being a doormat, it is a strong, seeking and seeing the heart of the Father's will and putting it into action kind of life. It is a life of actions of lovingkindness aligned to His heavenly will. Jesus, God the Father's only Son, was 'obedient unto death … of the cross' (Philippians 2:8, KJV) and sought to do only what He saw the Father do.[14]

When we surrender our lives to the Lord and know Him and walk with Him, in His way, truth and life, with His Holy Spirit continually, we will know how to please Him. Reading His words first and seeking His kingdom first every day unlocks the door to His heart. He affirms us through His Word, and we are able to die to our fleshy desires, leading us to a life which is alive in His living Holy Spirit. We also need to say 'No!' to our flesh and bad behaviour which does not align with our Father God's ways and commands. The late, great evangelist Reinhard Bonnke said:

14. John 5:19.

We have to say 'yes' to Jesus. Many have done that, but when saying 'yes' to Jesus, we must say at the same time 'no' to sin . . . We cannot walk in two directions at the same time.[15]

This rising up life is a life focused on God, who is good, who wants the best for us; a life which is pleasing to Him, which delights Him, a life of doing everything to Him and for Him in love, rather than a worldly focus on self. This chapter is a tiny glimpse of that which God teaches us about resurrection. It may not be easy, and it is often counter-cultural; however, the resurrection and a raised-up life is possible in Him.

One example of a humble life surrendered to the Lord who walked in Holy Spirit resurrection power is that of a simple man called William Seymour who was a pastor in the early twentieth century; he and his congregation experienced many years of miracle working revival at Azuza Street, which is still impacting generations of Christians today. He was described as 'humble', 'quiet' and 'soft spoken'. Theologian William Durham said of Seymour:

He walks and talks with God. His power is in his weakness. He seems to maintain a helpless dependence on God and is as simple-hearted as a child, and at the same time is so filled with God that you feel the love and power every time you get near him.[16]

---

15. Reinhard Bonnke, 'Reinhard Bonnke Tells of Nigerian Man Raised from the Dead', www2.cbn.com/article/salvation/reinhard-bonnke-tells-nigerian-man-raised-dead (accessed 15.1.24).
16. Shawn Stevens, 'William Durham, "A Chicago Evangelist's Pentecost"' (The Apostolic Faith, Vol. 1, No. 6, February-March 1907, Los Angeles: The Apostolic Faith Mission, p. 4), www.zionchristianministry.com/azuza/the-life-and-ministry-of-william-j-seymour (accessed 15.1.24).

It was said that William Seymour, this humble-hearted man, heard very clearly from God and was obedient, even to going into forbidden places which would have caused him harm if he were caught. He was a black man who obeyed God's instruction to go into a 'white' section of the city which was forbidden by racial rules at that time. As he obeyed God, risking his own life, many people were saved, healed and set free in the Glory cloud of God's blessing. Let us be inspired to practise being humble of heart; dependent on God, leading a life of resurrection power of God. The fruits of resurrection life are the love, glory and power of God.

Resurrection life every day

What does the Lord's resurrection life look like on earth? This book is a humble endeavour of discovery to find some of those answers. We need to be aware of Father God's will for each one of us in any given moment, through listening, hearing and submitting to His will on the matter. It is through a deep relationship of knowing our Father God, that we are able to live in resurrection life. It is to ask and seek and find God's views on every matter, little, big and everything in-between. This relationship grows over time and as we spend more time with our Father, Jesus and Holy Spirit daily through good times and bad. Becoming more mature in our Christlike walk, we know God's will as we have digested His words, and our spirit knows His spiritual ways. We have a knowing rather than a need to ask Him; in the same way a child learns and knows the best ways to go about life through an earthly parent. We grow spiritually and become close; yet have a holy awe and honour of God all at the same time.

In my first book, *Like Him*,[17] I write about giving up on our own efforts and relying on God's help. It is moments such as these which are resurrection moments:

My husband and I run a small business, and I have many testimonies about God's faithfulness and help. For example, I was responsible for recruitment, and I could not find the candidate we needed over many months. I gave up my own efforts after some hard trying. One day I decided to say a quick prayer: 'Help, Lord! Do You know anyone who would fit the bill?' God answered straightaway with a specific name. I was in the car at the time, so when I got home, I typed in the man's name in our recruitment database. Lo and behold, the chap was just the type of candidate I was searching for. I called him on the phone, and he was searching for a new position!'

Presently, this man is working for our family company, and (I hope!) his life has been changed for the better.

An aspect which will lead us away from a resurrected life, is the temptation in ourselves and from the enemy of our souls to idolise. Idol worship was one of the main issues which the children of Israel were guilty of and which brought the nation to disaster. 'Thou shalt have no other gods before me' (Exodus 20:3, KJV), says the Lord; this is the first commandment. We may think, 'Well, I do not have an idol in my life.' However, I believe idol 'worship' is more subtle than simply 'worshipping' an image. I was reading Habakkuk, in the context of living a righteous life, as instructed by the Holy Spirit and read:

---

17. Julia Stevens, *Like Him* (Southampton: Tree of Life, 2020), p. 108.

Woe to him who says to the wood, Awake! To the dumb stone, arise! It will teach ... there is no breath at all in the midst of it. But the LORD is in His Holy Temple! All the earth, Be silent before Him!

(Habakkuk 2:19-20)

There are things in our culture which can lead us into idol worship, if we are not careful to spend time with God, His Word and in prayer. For instance, overly watching the 'tell-a-vision' or media and receiving it's teaching and being influenced by its programmes and 'visions' as if they were 'the complete truth' daily.

Of what profit is the graven image that its maker has made it: ... a teacher of lies, that the maker of his work trusts in it ...   *(Habakkuk 2:18)*

Even our work itself can become an idol, if we place it in the centre of our lives, and wholeheartedly give ourselves to it, and believe teachings attached to it which are worldly; rather, we need to read and feed and believe the Word of God continually and walk by His Spirit. There are many examples of modern-day idols, such as: putting time on our mobile phone before time with Father God, giving more focus and time to our hobbies and putting them first in our lives before seeking after God and His plan for our lives. Anything which causes us to put our trust in our friends and even family more than God as our primary source of contentment, fulfilment of sin and worshipful focus is an idol: 'But seek ye first the kingdom of God, and his righteousness; and all these things [everything you need] shall be added unto you' (Matt 6:33, KJV). Ultimately focusing all your soul, strength and life on 'idols' leads to death rather than a resurrected life in God, which is the right life to live on earth.

The apostle Paul encourages us to pray continually and rejoice,[18] thanking God and listening carefully to His instruction both given into our hearts and via His Word as we meditate deeply on His words. There is joy in our journey as we focus on Father God, His middle name, after all, means 'laughter'! He is the God of Abraham, Isaac (meaning laughter) and Jacob!

A resurrected life in Messiah is one with no immoral behaviour; it is clean; it is a righteous life covered by the blood of Jesus. Paul explains that our bodies belong to God and need to be used righteously. We are encouraged by Paul to glorify our bodies as they belong to Father God. He writes that 'the Lord is for the body: and God even resurrected the Lord and He will resurrect us through His power. Do you know that your bodies are members of Messiah?' (1 Corinthians 6:13-15). The context of this scripture is concerning a case where a son was sexually immoral with his father's wife. Paul explains that when we behave immorally and unrighteously, we are joined to the world and reap its consequences of sin and therefore death: 'give such a one as this over to Satan [the enemy] for destruction of the flesh, so that his spirit could be saved in the Day of the Lord' (1 Corinthians 5:5) and urges us to 'flee immorality' (1 Corinthians 6:18). Paul declares: 'the unrighteous will not inherit the Kingdom of God' (1 Corinthians 6:9). These strong words are written in the book which also declares what love is: kind, compassionate, slow to anger and so on. Part of the Fatherly love of God is speaking the

---

18.   1 Thessalonians 5:16.

truth about the consequences of unrighteousness. The consequence of a righteous, faithful life in Father God is resurrection life; the consequence of an immoral life and immoral behaviour is destruction and death both spiritual and physical. We can repent, turn back to our Father through the Lord Jesus, who saves us from sin and eternal death. We can be saved to have a growing, loving, continual walk and relationship with the Lord.

The Lord has given us the choice whether to surrender to Him spiritually, speaking to us in our hearts, minds and bodies about His death and resurrection, and the two go together. We must die to self, in order to live in the resurrected life of love. Jesus is the divine authority over all things and you and I 'live and move and have our being' (Acts 17:28, NKJV) in Him. He has made us alive and has raised us up spiritually with Him, causing us to sit down in the heavenlies with Him. We are seated spiritually speaking, with Him at the right hand of our Father as His betrothed Bride.[19] All authority has been given to Him[20] and as we live and move and breathe in Him we have His authority, as he has given us the keys of the kingdom of heaven; whatever we 'bind on earth will be bound in heaven' and whatever we 'loose on earth will be loosed in heaven' (Matthew 16:19, NKJV). This is at the heart of the resurrected life on earth; living in His love and authority we are able to do the exploits He has asked us to do.

One of my mentors, Molly Sutherland, ran a ministry called Resurrected Life Ministries (mentioned above). She gave up hours of her time each week when she was in her mid-eighties, to bring sound biblical teaching and deep

19.   Romans 6:8; Ephesians 1:20; Ephesians 2:5-6; Colossians 3:3.
20.   Matthew 28:18.

healing ministry to hundreds of people. We prayed for each other during her sessions, and she prayed for the one whom God had purposed to heal that particular evening (we drew lots as the disciples did in Acts 1:26). Many have been transformed by her godly active, powerful teaching, prayer and washing feet at the bidding of Holy Spirit. For instance, I was delivered of a deep anger during one of these humbling sessions. We can be transformed by the Lord and His disciples by these acts of lovingkindness and tender mercies towards each other. Molly has since gone to be with her maker.

The Church and resurrection

The general subject of resurrection from the dead in the physical, spiritual and apocalyptic sense has not had the emphasis that it should have in the Western Church through the last decades. Our individual and corporate 'body' desperately needs more focus on resurrection generally, and obviously, particularly the resurrected life in Messiah Jesus. Why has this occurred? Some streams of the Church in the West have focused more on 'rapture', perhaps, if we are honest with ourselves, as an escape from the trials of this world, *rather* than resurrection. In my opinion, there has been a lack of faith caused by a reliance on medical science rather than biblical narrative and simple faith. Perhaps a lack of discipleship generally; a neglect of 'the Great Commission' teaching with which Jesus Christ instructed His disciples in Matthew 28. As indicated, a lack of sound teaching and preaching on the subject of resurrected life. All of these things and more may have contributed. Let us look together at resurrection and the resurrected life to redress this imbalance, if only a little.

Let us get back to the basic equation of faith:

Simple faith (in God's power and love) + simple obedience (to God's commands) = the tremendous miracle of resurrection life in The Lord God Almighty.[21]

Arise

In the beginning, the first mention in Scripture of the root word 'arise'; 'raised up' or 'resurrect' is found in Genesis 4:8 where Cain 'rises up'[22] to kill Abel through his anger and jealousy. Our good God has enabled redemption of everything through the cross, blood, 'burial' and resurrection of His Son, Jesus. The first spilt human blood of Abel which cried out from the ground[23] was answered by Jesus Christ: '. . . the sprinkled blood [of Christ] that speaks a better word than the blood of Abel' (Hebrews 12:24, ESV).

What word does the blood of Jesus speak which is a better word? One word might be: 'Mercy' another may be 'Beloved'. The name 'David' means 'beloved' and it always reminds me of the Bride of Christ, i.e. the one true

21. Mel Tari, *The Gentle Breeze of Jesus* (Lancashire: New Leaf Press, 1978).
22. Strong's H6965, www.blueletterbible.org/lexicon/h6965/kjv/wlc/0-1/ (accessed 29.1.24).
     Jeff A. Benner, 'While the word "resurrection" does not appear in English translations of Old Testament, it does appear in the New Testament as a translation for the Greek word αναστασις (*anastasis*, Strong's #386). This noun is derived from the word ανιστημι (*anistemi*, Strong's #450), which means "to stand up" or "to rise up."' Other source: 'In Modern Hebrew, the word for "resurrection" is המוקת (*tequmah*). This word is derived from the verbal root מוק (Q.W.M, Strong's #6965) meaning "to stand up" or "to rise up." The word המוקת (*tequmah*) is found in the Hebrew Bible. *And they shall stumble one upon another, as it were before the sword, when none pursueth: and ye shall have no power to stand before your enemies.* (ASV Leviticus 26:37)...ancient understanding of the "resurrection of the dead," is the "rising up of the dead," or more literally, the "standing up of the dead."' See www.Ancient-Hebrew.org (accessed 15.1.24).
23. Genesis 4:10.

Ekklesia or 'Church of God'.[24] Jesus' blood speaks of a new covenant, a new promise of relationship restored to Father God through Jesus, His Son, which enables a betrothal of the Bride; His *Ekklesia*, to be forever covenanted with Him in fullness of peace and perfect love and authority by His Holy Spirit. We belong individually and corporately to the Lord Jesus as His body and therefore we can have faith that the Lord himself will care for, nourish and protect His own body on earth as it is in heavenly realms, as we walk in this resurrection faith, belonging to Him alone; walking in His love, power and sound mind.[25]

Jesus is our living Word of resurrection life, and the more we can live from His words, the better. The words we declare over someone, or something, as we go about our lives, are important for 'Death and life are in the power of the tongue' (Proverbs 18:21, ESV). Let us remember to use words full of biblical faith as we speak about others, and especially when we prophesy, let us declare words of resurrection life over each other.[26]

Jesus Himself showed us how to use powerful faith filled, Godly words in His ministry to resurrect the dead. When the word 'arise!' (H6965) is used by faith, through the name and blood of Jesus, it can be declared by believers for a miraculous resurrection occurrence.

'Young man I say to you, arise!' And the dead man sat up and began to speak.

(Luke 7:14-15, NASB)

---

24. Strongs #G1577, www.blueletterbible.org/lexicon/g1577/nasb20/mgnt/0-1/ (accessed 24.1.24). Author's note: The Greek word *Ekklesia* is the original word for 'Church' which is the English translation derived from the ancient Germanic word: 'Kirk'.
25. 2 Timothy 1:7.
26. Romans 12:6.

According to the Blue Letter Bible, King James Version, the second incidence of 'arise' found in the Bible is at Genesis 6:18, which writes of God's establishment or 'raising up' of a new covenant with Noah:

'With thee will I establish [raise up] my covenant and thou shalt come into the ark, thou, and thy sons, and thy wife and thy sons and thy son's wives'.[27]

So here God is showing us the arising of a new promise, a covenant for the entire human race through Noah and his family. Out of the cleansing waters of the flood came the arising of a new beginning, which began with a promise from God never to flood the earth and cause this widespread death in the same way again.

God's heart is to resurrect not just the individual, but a nation and the nations; a beautiful, perfect Bride under His Kingly rule and reign. His heart is for a perfect and holy and clean new beginning.

As I was reading Numbers 10:33–36 in my quiet time with the Lord, I found in these few verses the Lord's heart for 'arising', resurrection life for a whole nation:

> ... they departed from the mountain of the LORD for three days' journey and the Ark of the Covenant of the LORD went before them on the three days' journey, to search out a resting place for them. And the cloud of the LORD was over them by day, when they went out of the camp. And it was, when the Ark set forward that Moses said: '*Arise* LORD! Your enemies will be scattered and those who hate you will flee before You'. And when it rested, he said: 'Return, LORD, to the many thousands of Israel. (my italics)

---

27. www.blueletterbible.org/kjv/gen/6/1/s_6001 (accessed 15.1.24).

Here the Lord's presence is going out before the nation of Israel and searches for a 'resting place' for the people. The Lord himself searches on earth for a resting place, a people and a place for His presence to rest. A cloud of the Glory of the Lord was hovering over the people as they moved. What a comforting vision to behold. It reminds me of Psalm 91, and abiding 'under the shadow of the Almighty' (v. 1). It was when the people of God collectively arose and went out of the camp, following the presence of the Lord, that this cloud of the presence of the Lord covered them. Quite often the '*arising*' resurrection presence and power of the Lord works on and in us as we go 'out of the camp', following His presence. In this text, the nation of Israel came down from the mountain of the Lord to go out. When we go out into the unbelieving world, down into the valleys, we take His presence to a world needing the resurrection life of the Lord.

Moses prophetically declares to the Lord: 'Arise Lord! Your enemies will be scattered...' Moses had faith and such a close relationship with the Lord, he could ask the Lord to 'arise' so that the works of the enemy would be destroyed.

When an individual is raised from the dead, the deathly works of the enemy are destroyed, and the living presence of the Lord Jesus Messiah intervenes. It is His presence which causes us to *arise* and thereafter causes those in the darkness to see a great light![28] In Isaiah 9:1-2, it is written:

The people who were walking in darkness have seen a great Light. The Light has shone upon those who dwell in the land of the shadow of death ... You have multiplied the nation, You have increased their joy. They rejoice before You according to the joy in harvest ...

---

28. Ephesians 5:14.

Let us follow the instructions in the Word of God, by His Spirit. When you hear His voice, 'Go!' And when you hear Him say 'Stay', do likewise.

Resurrection testimony

My dad was following the prompting of the Lord Jesus' lead when he prayed for a man in a restaurant. The following is his testimony of what happened in my dad, David Benson's own words:[29]

Some years ago, I went on holiday to Portugal with my wife, Mary, [and] our youngest daughter, Jessica, who was a teenager at the time. One day we went to a restaurant for lunch. It was a lovely sunny day, so we chose a table outside in the shade. We studied the menu, placed our order and settled down with some drinks.

There were many people passing close by and it was interesting just chatting away and watching the crowds of people out walking. This included many families, some holidaymakers and locals from Portugal itself.

I noticed a fairly large family which consisted of an older couple and their grown-up family, probably a half a dozen or so people. I saw that the younger ones were looking very worried about the older man, who didn't look well, and they were trying to comfort him.

At that point our food was brought out on a trolley by a waiter and placed on our table.

Suddenly, there was a screaming coming from the family and the older man disappeared from sight as

---

29. Edited for the purposes of this book.

he fell to the ground. I noticed one of the men was worriedly speaking on a mobile phone.

Without a further thought I got up and pushed my way through the crowd and got to the man who was lying on his back, completely still. His eyes were open but frozen and his face had turned white. To be honest he looked dead.

I immediately bent down and laid a hand on his forehead, commanding death to leave him and life to return to him, in Jesus' Name. Amen!

The family were in such turmoil, so I just pushed my way through and went back to our table and sat down. As I did so an ambulance turned up. Shortly afterwards the man, whom I prayed for, appeared, being carried by two men on a stretcher towards the ambulance. He was amazingly sitting up, looking over to me with a smile on his face.

There were two ladies sitting by a table next to us and cried out loud: 'What did you do? That man died?' We then testified all about Jesus and how he can raise people from the dead. Hallelujah!

So, there was a double blessing. The first blessing – was a man brought back to life and healed. The second blessing – that the two ladies were witnesses to what happened and we were able to testify all about our amazing Jesus Christ, healer and Saviour.

3

Resurrection Miracles of Jesus

Gripping her [firmly] by the hand, He said to her,
'Talitha cumi' – which translated is, Little girl,
I say to you, arise [from the sleep of death]!
(Mark 5:41, AMP)

Jesus is the focus of true resurrection life. He came to earth for you and me, to die and rise again, and has left His powerful Holy Spirit with us to continually in-fill His people. Jesus is the 'Resurrection and the Life' (John 11:25). A perfect 'place' to learn about resurrection is through the resurrection miracles of Jesus before he died and rose again. There are three accounts of resurrection achieved during Jesus' three-year ministry: Lazarus, Jairus' daughter and a young man raised at his own funeral. We can learn from these; and remember that it is the here and now, present reality of our relationship with the risen, victorious Christ through His powerful Holy Spirit that enables us to still see miracles today.

Nain

The miracle of Nain, in Luke's Gospel (7:11–17), is the story of a young man, the only son of a widow, who was raised up at his own funeral:

... As he approached the town gate, a dead person was being carried out—the only son of his mother, and she was a widow. And a large crowd from the town was with her. When the Lord saw her, his heart went out to her and he said, 'Don't cry.' Then he went up and touched the bier they were carrying him on, and the bearers stood still. He said, 'Young man, I say to you, get up!' The dead man sat up and began to talk, and Jesus gave him back to his mother ... (NIV)

This miracle must have greatly affected all the people in this small town. The raising from the dead occurred near to the gate. In those days, the elders' meetings were held at the town gate; perhaps such a meeting was beautifully interrupted by this miracle. Can you imagine, the news must have spread far and wide; soon the whole town would have known that the boy was no longer dead but alive. Glory to God!

It is interesting that Jesus encouraged the lady not to weep. He was going to cause the boy resurrection life, which may remind us of God's future promise of His kingdom, to: 'wipe away every tear from [our] eyes' (Revelation 7:17). God's resurrection power and love has the ability to wipe away our tears and bring joy for us on earth as it is in the heavenly realms, where there is the resurrection life of everlasting perfect peace ruling and reigning. I believe testimony of resurrection life helps to 'wipe away' those tears. Testimony brings hope, a smile to our face, joy to our hearts and a remembrance of God's heavenly happenings in our lives.

Jairus

Jairus, a synagogue's official, begged Jesus to go and help, as his daughter was very sick – dying. Jesus was delayed on the way when another miracle occurred due to the bold faith of a woman who was healed of an issue of blood: 'Daughter, take courage; your faith has made you well' (Matthew 9:22, NASB).

Jairus was told that his daughter had just died, causing the whole household to weep mournfully. However, Jesus encouraged Jairus' faith, saying: 'only believe' (Mark 5:36, ESV). This saying has echoed down through history. 'Only believe!' was preached by the famous Smith Wigglesworth, who had a great faith healing, miracle ministry and it is told that he saw at least fourteen people raised from the dead.[30] Let us follow Jesus' words and the example of those like Him who have gone before us and 'Only Believe!' in the power, love and resurrection life of Jesus, Father and Holy Spirit.

In the testimony story of Jairus' daughter, Jesus thereafter simply said: 'Talitha cumi!', which means 'Little girl, arise' or 'little girl, resurrect'. The Jewish official Jairus, whose name means 'enlightened', was truly enlightened as he saw his daughter raised from the dead.

Two thousand years later, holy people of God have been believing in the resurrection power of God. Here follows an account of one of the resurrection testimonies witnessed by Smith Wigglesworth, who 'truly believed':[31]

---

30. https://healingandrevival.com/BioSWigglesworth.htm
31. George Stormont, *Smith Wigglesworth: A Man Who Walked with God* (Tulsa, OK: Harrison House, 2019).

Resurrection testimony

'She [Mary Pople] told Bishop Ron Coady, and his wife of being paralyzed from the waist down in 1922 and being seriously ill. Wigglesworth was holding meetings in her town, and her friends urged her to let them take her to the meeting for prayer. However, she did not believe in divine healing and did not wish to be prayed for.

She soon became worse and, in fact, was dying. Her friends asked her if she would allow the evangelist to pray for her if they brought him to the house. She finally consented, but he was delayed. Before he arrived, she died.

Sister Mary Pople related that she went to heaven and was allowed in the throne room. She saw the Lord Jesus sitting on His throne. She saw the light such as she had never seen and heard music such as she had never heard before. Her heart was filled with rapturous joy.

As she looked at the Lord, He pointed to the doorway by which she had entered, and she knew she had to go back even if she did not want to. When she went through that door, she heard a voice that later she knew was Smith Wigglesworth's. He was saying, 'Death, I rebuke you in the name of Jesus.' Then he commanded Mary to live.

Her eyes opened, and those who had been weeping around her bed began to rejoice. She rose and dressed, and there was a knock at the door. Some girls from her Bible study group had arrived, thinking she was dead. To their surprise and joy, Mary herself opened the door to them.

She continued in the Lord's service for many years. Not only was she raised from the dead, but she was totally healed of her sickness that had been unto death and of the paralysis that had bound her for years.'

'Without faith it is impossible to please Him.'

(Hebrews 11:6, NKJV)

Translated

In every time and era, there are accounts of people who are miraculously saved from certain death and the following is an account where the Lord God steps in to save a young man. Matthew is a friend from Living Word Church, Fareham, Hampshire and during dinner he shared with me his own 'raised up' experience as follows:[32]

I was called over to a table where Matthew was sharing 'the reason I found God'. He was on holiday for the day in and around Acapulco's beaches many years ago . . . in his late twenties. He was there for a day only and remembers being told not to go into the sea at certain points. Being an adventurous sort and wanting to cool off, Matthew ventured into the sea anyway. He was soon remembering the warnings given him, when he found himself out in the depths of the ocean, unable to swim back to the shore. He kept afloat for a time with his own strength, but remembers becoming extremely exhausted after a long while, with no one around to come to his aid. It was at this point that he decided within himself to 'give up', to surrender

---

32. Drowning testimony from Living Word Church, Fareham at Sunday Meal, January 2023, written by author. Edited for the purposes of this book.

himself up to death . . . We were eagerly waiting for what would happen next, listening intently to his story. He told us that he said in his heart: 'I give myself up to you now God, this is it!' He thought he was at death's very door as he sank into the sea. The very next moment . . . he found himself washed up on the actual beach again. He cannot explain what happened, only that God must have either translated him back to shore, or some sort of other angelic intervention had saved his life that day. After this happening, Matthew has followed God the Father, Jesus Christ and Holy Spirit ever since, knowing that he had, and is still, being saved.

4

Resurrection Foretold

'Sir . . . tell me where you have laid Him,
and I will take Him away.'
Jesus said to her, 'Mary!'
She turned and said to Him, 'Rabboni!'
(which is to say, Teacher)
(John 20:15–16, NKJV)

Before He was killed on a cross, Jesus let His friends, His disciples and even crowds of people, know that He was to rise again. I counted at least seventeen instances where Jesus told or showed His disciples or the crowd that 'after they scourge Him they will kill Him, and on the third day He will be raised' (Luke 18:33), or similar phrases stating that He would die and then rise. Yet, His resurrection was a surprise to them for a few reasons. Jesus invariably spoke in the third person about Himself, or in a parable.

The language and phrases Jesus used were not as clear to some as to others. Jesus spoke in parables. For example, in Matthew 26:61, Jesus speaks of the temple being torn down and built up again in three days as a metaphor for His death and resurrection. He also speaks of Himself being in the belly of the earth, likening himself to Jonah, addressing Himself as: 'the Son of Man' being in 'the heart of the earth' for 'three days and three nights' (Matthew 12:40). He was showing them that this part of the story of Jonah was a living prophetic foreshadow of that which would happen to Him, our incredible Messiah. Perhaps many did not realise the meaning in His parabolic way of speaking about future events?

It is written in Luke 18:34 that even His disciples did not sometimes understand clearly that which Jesus spoke of. However, John is kinder and writes that after the resurrection, the disciples remembered and believed the 'Scripture and the words which Jesus had said' (John 2:22, NKJV). So, what is the truth about that which they generally perceived beforehand?

Let us think about how you and I perceive and hear 'The Word of the Lord'. Admittedly, at times we have not listened carefully to what the Lord is saying. Let us be careful to listen and ask for understanding, for revelation, wisdom and clarity from the Lord. We can ask questions of Him, like a child to their father; this is a good place to begin. If the Lord tells you something, or shows you something, ask questions around it: is there anything you want me to do, Lord? Thank Him, and ask Him to show you what the implication, context or reason is for that which He told you. I pray you will hear and be led by His Spirit.

In Luke 9, Jesus foretells His death and resurrection a couple of times, and in verse 45 it is written that Jesus says the disciples did not understand the meaning of His words because it had been hidden from them, and they were afraid to ask for clarification.

But they did not understand this statement, and it was *concealed* from them so that they would not comprehend it; and they were afraid to ask Him about this statement.

(Luke 9:45, NASB, my italics)

The Greek wording for 'concealed' is 'parakalupto'. This verb is passive, which infers that the disciples were not the cause of this concealment, but that God 'concealed' it from them. We wonder, why God caused them *not* to understand? Could it be possible the disciples would have done something that was not the will of The Father, if they had clarity?[33] We know that some of the disciples such as Simon the Zealot were trained in the things of war and others such as Judas Iscariot were thinking that Jesus the Messiah had come to save the Jews, and indeed the world, from the Roman Empire's tyranny, through building a victorious physical army. However, God's ways are higher than humankind's and His thoughts are higher, as we read in Isaiah 55:9. Jesus had come to do battle in a different way; triumphing over the spiritual world through His sacrificial love and resurrection power, which enables us to have His mind on every matter, should we listen, seek and obey His right way.

Father God sometimes conceals things from us until we are mature enough to seek His will on the matter; let us admit we might at times take things into our own hands, and action things which are not in God's wider plan. Even Abraham sought to bring forth God's promise through Hagar before God's timing. God knows that we might do something foolish if we knew more than we can handle about the future, as we read in Genesis 16. We can trust

---

33. www.neverthirsty.org/bible-studies/ministry-perea/death-resurrection-of-jesus-prophesied/ (accessed 15.1.24).

Father God by His Holy Spirit to reveal things to us in due time. Let us commune with Him as to His will on any matter when we hear news, good and bad. We can rest and trust that Father God has a sovereign plan. Let us ask Him our part to achieve in His plans.

Do we really *know*?

In Luke 20:37, Jesus gives a wonderful answer to the Sadducees, who ask Him about resurrection in the context of marriage: 'Who would be a husband in the afterlife of a wife of many husbands?' (my paraphrase), they asked. After stating clearly that there is no such thing as marriage in the way we have on Earth, in Heaven; Jesus intimates that Abraham, Isaac and Jacob are already 'raised' and living in the afterlife. He says: 'Now He is not the God of the dead, but of the living; for all live to Him' (Luke 20:38, NASB).

Like the Sadducees, the disciples of Jesus may not have had a correct theology or concept of 'The Resurrection of the Messiah'. For instance, they may have thought of Jesus being raised from the dead at some point in future, and not thought of His appearing to them after the three days He spoke of. They may have thought he would appear to His Father God in heaven, but not necessarily come to them on earth after His raising. Many times, we too might misunderstand or have a wrong theology or concept of some of the things which are written in Scripture; however, we can thank God in faith that the Holy Spirit will reveal things to us clearly when the appointed time is right.

Let us thank God now and ask Holy Spirit for more clarity of the prophesy in the living Word left to be fulfilled; especially, I believe, for the last days that we are now living in. We want to be prepared for the things ahead. God our Father, through His Holy Spirit will help us be prepared, our part is seeking the truth of His kingdom and righteousness.[34]

The resurrection of Jesus

Jesus' resurrection was different to all previous resurrections and raisings from the dead. He is the 'Firstborn of all creation' (Colossians 1:15) who is holy and lived a sinless holy life; He is begotten, not created. He is the second Adam, who took away the sin of the world. When He rose, unlike Lazarus, who we read about in John 11, He did not rise to die again; He rose once and for all to ascend to His Father's throne in the heavenly realms so that we would be able to rise and to ascend with Him and spiritually be seated with Him. He left us His Holy Spirit on earth, His breath of life. Ultimately, those who overcome are called to rule and reign with Jesus as His Bride: The New Jerusalem will come down from heaven to the new earth.[35]

The apostle Peter shows us that Jesus' resurrection was foretold in the Old Testament scripture. Peter addresses the Jews after Pentecost, quoting Psalm 16:8-10:

I have set the LORD always before me;
because he is at my right hand, I shall not be shaken.
Therefore my heart is glad, and my whole being rejoices;
my flesh also dwells secure.
For you will not abandon my soul to Sheol,
or let your holy one see corruption.

(ESV)

---

34. Matthew 6:33.
35. 'And I saw the holy city, new Jerusalem, coming down out of heaven from God, made ready as a bride adorned for her husband' (Revelation 21:2, NASB).

In these last days of our era, as I believe them to be, it is important to digest, to meditate day and night, in the Word of God. I found another prophetic picture of the resurrection of Messiah Jesus in Hosea 6:2 as I was doing just this: 'After two days He will revive us: on the third day He will raise us up and we will live in His sight.' How wonderful that the resurrection of our Messiah is foretold and that we are the people He died and rose again for, that we might be raised up and live in His sight to worship Him forever. Thank You, Lord, that You watch over us. Interestingly, the above verse could also be applied to the revelation prophecy of the two witnesses' resurrection which we will explore later in this book.

In summary, our Messiah Jesus' resurrection was foretold in the Old Testament in many scriptures. For example, Paul writes in Acts 2:31 that King David prophesied Jesus Messiah's coming, saying that, concerning the resurrection of the Messiah: '"neither would He be forsaken in Hades nor" His flesh "see corruption"' in Psalm 16:10.

Jesus told His disciples many times that He would rise again after being killed. The religious leaders of Jesus' day did not believe and/or misunderstood the Old Testament prophesies about Messiah's death and resurrection. Father God concealed even Jesus' own words from His disciples. Jesus' resurrection was a surprise to many; except our Father God in heaven and perhaps one or two closest in relationship to Jesus. I would surmise the same will happen on His second coming; those who are surrendered to Him, close to Him, are baptised and full of His Holy Spirit, having the privilege of knowing the times and the season – they are the prepared remnant, Bride of the Messiah robed in His righteousness, peace and joy. Let us ready ourselves together, Bride of Messiah, for He is coming soon.

Resurrection testimony

Sharing testimonies with each other helps us to be overcomers and to be encouraged in His hope and faith. In Dr Rex Gardner's case studies of miracles from *A Doctor Investigates Healing Miracles*,[36] he writes about a few resurrection testimonies including the following account:

> The case I know of resurrection from the dead took place in the country district of Salta Pura, which is several kilometres from Nueva Imperial in the ninth region. It was when Andres Montupil, a Mapuche evangelist . . . visited a very hard area. He had drink thrown over him and a remark: 'If you want to do anything with your message, there is someone who needs you over yonder.' . . . there was a child, 13 or 14 years old who was very ill. And so Andres found his way to the haystack-like house. He knew he had come to the right one because the howling of uncontrollable grief and hopelessness could be heard. It was a Mapuche woman grieving at the time of death.
>
> I understand that Andres drew near the house praying very much and went in and comforted the woman in the usual way. He was able to very gently lead her outside the house to where there was a clear view of the mountains, and was able to say, 'My Father made this, and your Father too, and he has power to raise up your daughter who is dead, and we are going to pray.' He returned to the house. The child was still lying on the bed where she had just died. Everyone

36. Rex Gardner, *A Doctor Investigates Healing Miracles* (London: Darton, Longman & Todd, 1986). With permission from Will Parkes, 2/8/23PR/ Marketing/Rights/Permissions/Royalties/e-Publishing Darton, Longman & Todd, 1 Spencer Court, 140-142 Wandsworth High St, London, SW18 4JJ www. dltbooks.com @dlt_books

was distraught. She was by now cold and stiffening. Andres took off his coat to get down to prayer and he said: 'We all prayed and nothing happened and the second time we all prayed again and nothing happened.'

And he said the third time: 'Lord, for your glory, so the people know you exist and that you have power, raise their daughter.' And the third time she coughed, moved and there was life. Andres was able to call for something to be given her to eat, thin soup. He stayed in the home for two or three days teaching them about the Lord. Some neighbours came for the wake and found the child awake. The family came to know the Lord and a church was formed. [Miss Clark concludes:] 'I subsequently met the girl and the family and the church...' Halleluyah!

5

Resurrections Retold

———◆———

My testimony true
I had once died.
Now made alive,
To serve a-new,
One sacrificed.
Once for all,
Life eternal.

Authentic testimony, witness and re-telling of true stories are an essential aspect of our faith as this builds the Church individually and corporately. There were witnesses to most experiences written in this book, who could testify to the reality of what happened during the raising of the dead and, as a result, other people have been greatly and positively affected. The same situation occurs with most biblical accounts we read; two or more witnesses have verified these histories. We have chosen sources which are people of good character and those who have undergone godly transformation in their lives as a result. The fruit of their experience remains; that is, more often than not, a moral and surrendered life of continued devotion to the Lord God and to Jesus Christ.

Generally speaking, our western 'scientific' culture seeks to explain away resurrection from the dead and is, on the whole, sceptical; however, there are many miracles of resurrection which still go wholly unexplained. During research for this book, I came across some of these modern resurrection testimonies.

One of the books of testimony I admire, and which I encourage you to read, is Dr Craig Keener's book *Miracles Today*[37] and particularly Part Five: 'The Dead Are Raised', where he outlines many resurrection testimonies, including a number of true stories from the Western world. He details testimony of doctors who have witnessed people raised from the dead as well as experiences of his own friends and family being 'Raised Up'. Dr Keener, from Asbury University, also relates resurrection testimonies in an article discussing resurrection miracles in the magazine *Christianity Today* and he has given me permission to paraphrase his writings.[38] Here is my paraphrase of some of these true stories:

A two-year-old girl called Thérèse was bitten by a snake in the Republic of Congo. Her mother, Antoinette, rushed to her side. However, Thérèse was not responding and seemed to have stopped breathing. There was no medical help available in their village, so strapping Thérèse onto her back in a sling, Antoinette ran quickly to a nearby village.

I learned from Dr Keener that brain cells begin to die less than five minutes after the oxygen supply is removed from the person, this is called 'hypoxia'. Apparently, it takes just six minutes of lack of oxygen to cause severe brain damage or brain death. It took Antoinette about three hours to reach the next village. When they arrived, Thérèse

---

37. Keener, *Miracles Today*.
38. Keener, 'Real Raisings from the Dead or Fake News?' Permission given by Dr Keener to paraphrase his words.

was, according to medical science, most likely either dead or had sustained significant brain damage.

Coco Ngoma Moyise, a friend, prayed over the lifeless girl. Immediately she came to life, breathing again. The following day, she was completely well and had recovered – no sign of long-term illness and no brain damage whatsoever. To this day, Thérèse is well, she has a Master's degree and is a pastor in Congo.

Dr Keener testified that he was sceptical when he first heard of this story – it was ultimately difficult to deny though, as Thérèse is his sister-in-law and the mother, Antoinette is his own mother-in-law!

Another testimony which Dr Keener relates is as follows – again, in my own words:

A Nigerian friend whom Dr Keener worked with called Leo Bawa, who was a missions' researcher and now holds a PhD from the Oxford Centre for Mission Studies. During research for a book on miracles, Keener asked Bawa if he knew of any miracles. He replied that there weren't many; he then proceeded to give Keener seven pages of eyewitness accounts!

One of these miracle experiences was in a village where some non-Christian neighbours brought Bawa their dead child, asking if he could help them. He prayed for a few hours and then handed the child back to them alive. Keener, thinking it may have been a misdiagnosed death, asked how often Bawa had prayed for dead people to rise again. He said he had done so only one other time. He had prayed for his best friend after he had died, and the friend had remained dead. In this non-Christian village, however, Bawa believes God answered his prayer that day, for the glory and honour of Christ, to show the unbelievers the glory of God.

Another raising from the dead which Dr Keener relates is the account of a Nigerian man, whom he met from his time in Africa during research days. Some years later, Keener's medical doctor and mutual friends told of this man's resurrection testimony. Keener followed up on his story. It was in December 1985 that the man was killed in a head-on traffic accident. After being pronounced dead on arrival in the hospital, he was sent to the morgue. Many hours later, as a worker went in to move some of the bodies; he found the body moving. The doctor at the hospital expected that the man would at least have irreparable brain damage due to lack of oxygen. But he fully recovered; something his maxilla-facial surgeon described as nothing short of 'miraculous'. Nowadays, this man is an Anglican priest and a leader in the Nigerian missions' movement.

Dr Keener's book emphasises accounts of medics and highly credible witnesses to resurrection experiences, as this offers more credibility. He gives many examples of testimony from people who are highly academic. For example, he was in an academic meeting with a man who has a PhD from the University of Manchester, and he began sharing some global miracle accounts he had been collecting for his book. A few Western professors in the meeting questioned him about these testimonies. In the discussion, the man stood up, giving his own experience on the subject. He testified that his own son was pronounced dead at birth in 1981. After half an hour of prayer, however, the child was restored with no brain damage. This same son now has a Master's degree from University College London and another from Cornell.

6

Lazarus is Raised Up!

———◆———

Laid down to sleep,
Mourners weep
Believing in The Way
Resurrection on The Final Day
And how about right now?
Will our faith allow?
The dead to be raised up.

During Jesus' day, resurrection was not a strange idea to the Jewish people. In John 11:24 Martha says to Jesus that she knows that her brother will be resurrected 'on the last day' (ESV). Lazarus, Jesus' good friend, was raised up, as we read in John 11.

Lazarus means 'God helps', or 'God is my helper'. This reminds us of the role of the Holy Spirit, our great helper, who was sent at Pentecost after Jesus had ascended to be with the Father God. In John 16:7-8, Jesus said it was better that He went away as he would send the Holy Spirit to help bring righteousness and justice on the earth. It is the powerful, glorious Holy Spirit who enables the raising of the dead to occur in our times.

In John 11, Jesus told His disciples of Lazarus that he was asleep and that he would go to awaken him. Perhaps when we think of 'sleeping and awakening' when thinking about resurrecting the dead, it can give us more faith and puts things into more of a heavenly context. The heavenly context is that raising the dead is as simple and 'ordinary' to the faith-filled Christian man or woman as an awakening from sleep. Having simple faith, like a child, enables us to bring resurrection life into a dark world.

Jesus deliberately delayed getting to Lazarus in the account of his being raised from the dead. Jesus was also delayed in the account of Jairus' daughter. Both accounts brought glory to the Lord and more disciples were made through the resurrection of Lazarus: many believed. This reminds us that God's ways are higher than ours. Lazarus' family thought the Lord God had forgotten them, or that God was too late. It seems as though Jesus was 'late' due to the purposes of God, our Father, in order that a resurrection would occur, and the glory of Father God could be displayed even more brightly for the sake of the world (John 11:15). We have been waiting for the return of Jesus, our Messiah, for a good while and the hour seems late. In the waiting we can be thankful and rejoice that the full number of people will be brought to salvation due to the timing of God's grace.

The resurrection of Lazarus is a type of foreshadowing of the resurrection of Jesus. Jesus Himself was raised after a few days. In John's account of Lazarus, 'Jesus wept' (v. 35), perhaps foreseeing His own cruel death. He also 'groans' within himself a couple of times (see verses 33 and 38), interceding with 'groanings too deep for words' (Romans 8:26, ESV) as well as foreseeing His own ordeal to come. He then says to Mary, Lazarus' sister: 'I AM the Resurrection and the Life: the one who believes in Me, even if he would die, he will live' (John 11:25).

These powerful words that Jesus spoke, which speak directly into our heart and mind, show us that when we believe in Jesus as God, the God of resurrection life itself, we are saved, healed, forgiven and can receive His Holy Spirit of resurrection life. When we are baptised by His Spirit, fire and water, we bubble up and share this raised-up life within us with others around us. We are restored by the river of His Words and Spirit and are enabled to restore others. We can pray in His power, by His name and blood, and through Him, raise the dead back to life! Amen.

After the resurrection of Lazarus, in John 12, Jesus and Lazarus are seen at the same gathering. People came to the gathering so that they could see Lazarus whom Jesus had raised from the dead, perhaps to see if the rumours were true? In verse 3, it is written that a woman poured out 'costly pure nard ointment' on Jesus' feet during this gathering. Here there is a link to Song of Songs, with this outpouring of fragrant oil: 'Your name is as ointment poured forth, therefore the young maidens do love You.' This is an outpouring of true love upon our Bridegroom Jesus, whose name is above all names and who was receiving a prophetic love anointing from His Bride, who was preparing His body for the ordeal on the cross: 'Let her alone,' Jesus says, 'she has kept this for the day of My burial' (John 12:7, NKJV).

As the body of Messiah, it is these deep outpourings of love for Jesus, our Bridegroom, and for each other, from the Holy Spirit, which also help us through our ordeals and trials we face. Jesus' body was prophetically anointed before His death; another witness to everyone present at the gathering that He is truly Messiah, the Anointed One.[39]

The religious leaders attended this gathering also and they wanted to kill Lazarus as well as Jesus, because many

---

39. The word 'anointed' or Mashiach in Hebrew means to be smeared with oil; this is where the word Mashiach, Messiah or Christ comes from www.blueletterbible.org/lexicon/h4886/nasb20/wlc/0-1/ (accessed 29.1.24).

were believing that He was the Messiah. Wherever there is true resurrection life and testimony, there is an enemy who wants to 'kill' the testimony and also the life of the resurrected one. However, due to the death, resurrection and ascension of Jesus, our Messiah, He that is in us has power and authority over the enemy who comes against the resurrection life Himself: Jesus. We are covered by His blood and filled with His living Spirit of life. All authority is given to us 'in heaven and upon the Earth', as it is to Jesus (Matthew 28:18-19). We are covered by His blood and by the faith we have in Him. Whatever we loose on earth will be loosed in heaven and vice versa.[40] We are equipped by the Lord's authority to destroy the evil works of the enemy.

Jesus was led on a colt into Jerusalem on account of people testifying about the resurrection of Lazarus.[41] They cried out: 'Hoshea-na!' or 'Save us now!' as Jesus rode into the holy city. The crowd proclaimed Him 'the King of Israel' (John 12:13, KJV). They may not have realised that this King of all would die and rise to deliver them of their sin and send His Holy Spirit to enable them to follow Him to be Christ-ones. All these years later we, His beautiful Bride, are saved and are enabled to walk this life in His resurrected power and love. Praise Him!

Lazurus the beggar

The Bible gives account of two Lazarus' who died. The first one is related by Jesus in Luke 16 which is a proverb about a poor beggar called Lazarus who sat outside a rich man's house. The crux of the story shows that the unbelieving rich

40. Matthew 16:19; Matthew 18:18.
41. John 12:17.

man and family had no faith in an afterlife, and therefore: 'they will not [even] be persuaded if someone would rise from the dead' (Luke 16:31).

The two Lazarus accounts are linked. The religious rulers of Jesus' day behaved just like the rich man in Jesus' prophetic proverb from Luke. When they saw Lazarus of Bethany raised from the dead in such a dramatic way, they still did not choose to believe that Jesus was the Messiah, Son of God. No number of miraculous signs or wonders would cause them to believe. This is at the heart of unbelief. You must believe in Jesus as Christ and as God Himself, otherwise unbelief can creep into your mind and heart, causing death to the spirit. Let us choose eternal life and believe that Jesus is the Son of God.

The Lazarus of Jesus' parable was sent to Abraham's 'bosom' (Luke 16:23). There is also another term used in the Bible for a similar 'realm' which is found in the testimony of the thief who was crucified next to Jesus, who was told: 'today you will be with Me in Paradise' (Luke 23:43, NKJV). Is Paradise a waiting place for the righteous? Whether we are sent to Abraham's Bosom, or to Paradise, we need to make sure we seek after the truth and deepen our relationship with God. As my grandmother famously quoted: 'God knows' (2 Corinthians 12:3). God knows all truth; He sees everything and is all in all.

Lazurus of Bethany

The Pharisaic belief at the time of Lazarus was that on the fourth day of death, the spirit ascended to heaven. I wonder, did they forget that it is Father God who makes and thereafter implements the heavenly and earthly 'rules', not humankind? Perhaps this is why Jesus waited to raise Lazarus; to show them and indeed, us all: who truly makes the rules? And who decides those rules? The Lord, who has grace and mercy! This triumphs over judgement and legalism. The Lord God raises the dead today and it is He who judges concerning this incredible happening. Jesus' desire was to show the religious leaders that He is the true Messiah; the one who has power over death and Hades.

Some of the Pharisees of Jesus' time became disciples but many did not have faith in Jesus as Messiah, even though they witnessed Lazarus being raised from the dead after four days. It was due to their instruction and belief (a man or woman's spirit goes to Sheol on the 'fourth day')[42] that the unbelieving Pharisees were also blinded; preferring to stubbornly stick to their own beliefs than have an open heart and mind. Let us not assume or rely so much on the doctrine of humankind that we miss the glory of God. Let us read, meditate and contemplate the Word of God and walk in His Spirit daily.

Due to the real-life Lazarus of Bethany being raised from the dead, many Jews of the day *did* believe in Jesus and that He was and indeed is Messiah, Son of God, King of the universe, the question is for us today is: will we? And will we accomplish that which Jesus asked of His disciples?

---

42. 'J.P. Lange and P. Schaff, *A Commentary on the Holy Scriptures: John* (Bellingham, WA: Logos Bible Software, 2008). 'Jewish mysticism teaches that a deceased person's spirit remains around the body for up to three days after death before departing. It was well-known in Israel 2,000 years ago that someone deceased could come back to life during this 3-day period but not afterwards. On the fourth day, the spirit left the body and went to Sheol or Hades, and there was no hope for life without a miracle. Also, by the fourth day in Israel's hot climate, advanced decay would be destroying the body, and the stench would have been overwhelming. When Jesus called Lazarus to life from the dead and healed his rotted corpse, the people knew that He was the true Messiah, performing genuine miracles as the prophets had foretold!' https://hermeneutics.stackexchange.com/questions/39265/why-did-jesus-delay-four-days-in-going-to-the-tomb-of-lazarus (accessed 22.1.24).

Will we have faith and do the works of lovingkindness which He has called us to?

You must continually heal sicknesses, raise the dead, cleanse lepers, cast out demons: you took freely, you must now give freely.

(Matthew 10:8)

Resurrection testimony

Here is another amazing testimony to encourage your faith that the Lord is still raising the dead today, even in our western world.

Sandra's testimony:[43]

Sandra has passed into glory and the summer before she went to heaven, being in her late seventies, she related to me that when she was twenty-three years old, she experienced a coming back to life happening which would change her life forever, this is why she had such a strong faith. It was the late 1960s and Sandra was a qualified nurse out with her doctor and nurse colleagues who were also good friends. They were travelling in a car to Cambridge. The car stopped functioning while travelling at speed and began zigzagging all over the road. Every other passenger as well as the driver got out of the car relatively safely apart from Sandra. Her foot was caught under the front seat, and she was trying to wriggle it free but was not able to. She faced a full-on collision and

---

43. Via interview with the author in September 2022, Living Word Church, Fareham. Edited for the purposes of this book.

lost consciousness as the car crashed. She vaguely remembers some doctors coming to her aid. She was in and out of consciousness as they endeavoured to lift her.

Suddenly she saw a very bright white light and she felt a very strange sensation of being out of her body. She remembers being in a wonderfully peaceful place and seeing green grass and somebody's sandaled feet. She supposed immediately that it was Jesus. Sandra does not remember much else of this experience except that she then found herself back in her earthly body.

Afterwards, her trainee doctor and nurse friends, who were all safe and sound, though shaken and shocked after the accident, all agreed that they saw two male truckers on the scene who got there before anyone else, who may have prayed for her; though they disappeared quickly from the scene once the medics arrived.

Sandra was in hospital for a short time with a slight fracture and twisted foot and recovered fully from this head-on collision.

Her mother told her that she too had a similar back to life experience, and that she also was not now afraid to die and cross over into, as she believed, heavenly eternity.

Resurrection gives us all faith, boldness and courage. Sandra told me that the main effect of her experience was that she now knows she need not be afraid to die, nor of death itself. Sandra passed into heaven in September 2023 and is missed on earth, but we imagine that she is truly happy in heaven.

7

Resurrection Day – He is Risen!

He, Christ, lays down His life,
He has the power to take it again;
and the veil rent,
for the mysterious doors of Heaven are opened;
the rocks are cleft, the dead arise.
He dies, but he gives life,
and by His death, destroys death.
He is buried, but He rises again.
He goes down to Hell,
but He brings up the souls;
He ascends to Heaven,
and shall come again to judge the quick and the dead.

Gregory of Nazianzus (AD 330–389)[44]

As Christ followers, we have such a wonderful hope because of Jesus' resurrection from the dead. Jesus has given us a continual *living* hope. The Gospel accounts of the Lord Jesus rising again and their credibility to the believer are of paramount importance to our faith, and everything surrounding His resurrection is of significance.

According to the Jewish Messianic tradition, Jesus rose again on the same day, thousands of years later, that

---

44. https://normangeisler.com/the-early-fathers-and-the-resurrection-of-the-saints-in-matthew-27/ (accessed 22.1.24).

Noah's ark rested on the earth again after the flood.[45] There is a beautiful meaning behind the name of 'Noah', which in Hebrew means 'comfort' and 'rest'. According to this tradition, on the day of the resting of the ark, our Saviour and Lord rose, enabling His beloved people to 'enter into the rest' of eternity here and now.

This is also the day known on the calendar as 'First Fruits', when the children of Israel were to bring the sacrifices of their first harvest to the Lord God after they entered the promised land. Clearly this is a day hand-picked by the Father God for His beloved Son to rise again from the dead. A day for a new beginning. This was a day chosen especially to show humankind that the Messiah has won victory over death through His blood sacrifice once and for all time! The only begotten Son of the Father God has triumphed over sin, death and hell on this most special of days.

Paul speaks of Jesus Messiah as being:

> ... the first fruits of those who have fallen asleep. For as by a man came death, by a man has come also the resurrection of the dead. For as in Adam all die, so also in Christ shall all be made alive, first fruits of those who have slept. For since death is through a man, then resurrection of the dead is through a Man. Just as all are dying in Adam, So, also will all be made alive in Christ.
>
> *1 Corinthians 15:20–22*

45. www.thebiblecanbeproven.com (accessed 15.1.24).

Resurrection at Jesus' death

An amazing first fruits of a 'raised up' harvest happened at Jesus' resurrection when many saints arose from their graves when Jesus rose again:

> The tombs were opened, and many bodies of the saints who had fallen asleep were raised; and coming out of the tombs after His resurrection, they entered the holy city and appeared to many.
>
> *(Matthew 27:52-53, NASB)*

The prophet Isaiah foretold this event in Isaiah 26:19:

> Your dead people will live. They will rise together with my dead body. Awake! Sing! You who dwell in dust, for your dew is like the dew of herbs, and the earth will cast out the dead.

This resurrection of the dead saints at Jesus' resurrection is a prophetic foreshadowing of the resurrection of *all* the saints in the last days. The resurrected saints in Matthew 27:53,[46] for instance, enter the holy city, appearing to many, which is the pattern of those resurrected at the end of times. In the book of Revelation, the overcoming saints enter the holy New Jerusalem: 'But you have come to Mount Zion and the city of the Living God, heavenly Jerusalem' (Hebrews 12:22). Many wonder what became of those saints who were resurrected with Jesus, and commentator Matthew Henry[47] gives us a probable answer:

---

46. 'The tombs also were opened. And many bodies of the saints who had fallen asleep were raised, and coming out of the tombs after his resurrection they went into the holy city and appeared to many. When the centurion and those who were with him, keeping watch over Jesus, saw the earthquake and what took place, they were filled with awe and said, "Truly this was the Son of God!"' (Matthew 27:52-54, ESV).
47. Matthew Henry commentary from the www.blueletterbible.org (accessed 11.10.23).

... it is more agreeable, both to Christ's honour and theirs, to suppose, though we cannot prove, that they arose as Christ did, to die no more, and therefore ascended with him to glory.

These righteous saints most likely ascended together with Jesus on Ascension Day, forty days after His resurrection.

In the Gospel of Nicodemus, a Pharisee whom Jesus encountered and with whom discussed death and everlasting life in John 3, details the event of people rising from the dead at Jesus' death. This is the account:

Then Rabbi Addas and Rabbi Finees, and Rabbi Egias, the three men who had come from Galilee, testifying that they had seen Jesus taken up into heaven, rose up in the midst of the multitude of the chiefs of the Jews, and said before the priests and the Levites, who had been called together to the council of the Lord: 'When we were coming from Galilee we met at the Jordan a very great multitude of men, fathers who had been some time dead' ... And they went and walked around all the region of the Jordan and of the mountains, and they were coming back without finding them. And, behold, suddenly there appeared coming down from Mount Amalek a very great number, as it were, twelve thousand men, who had risen with the Lord. And though they recognized very many there, they were not able to say anything to them for fear and the angelic vision; and they stood at a distance gazing and hearing them, how they walked along singing praises, and saying; 'The Lord has risen again from the dead, as He has said; let us all exult and be glad, since He reins for ever. [sic] Then those who had been sent were astonished and fell to the ground for fear, and received the answer from them, that they should see Karinus and Leucius in their own houses. And they rose up and went to their houses, and found them spending their time in prayer.[48]

The Tomb

The account of Jesus' resurrection in Luke 24, is shown by Luke primarily from the women's viewpoint. The Gospels indicate that Jesus was seen by women first after His death; this is a redemptive echo of all things being made new spiritually thousands of years after Eve first gave in to temptation from the enemy, her husband thereafter making the same choice, and consequently the Fall occurred, as we read in Genesis 3. Mary of Magdala, saved and delivered of 'seven demons' (Luke 8:2), was the first to witness the risen Jesus in a garden where the tomb was situated. Both the Fall and the saving grace of resurrection life were both witnessed in a garden.

Let us take a moment to meditate on Luke's account of resurrection and use it to bring a new focus on Jesus' resurrection power. We can look at this testimony from a spiritual point of view for ourselves. The story begins with the women coming to the tomb early with spices to clean and prepare the body; they may have forgotten about His words to them that he would be raised from the dead. They expected to tend to His body with ritual preparations'.

. . . on the first day of the week, at early dawn, the women went to the tomb, bringing the spices which they had prepared [to finish anointing the body].

(Luke 24:1, AMP)

---

48. *The Gospel of Nicodemus*, Vol. 8, Chapter 1.

In a similar way, you and I can bring our own old, perhaps empty religious, ritualistic ways of doing things, and bring them to Jesus; seeing Him dead on the cross, instead of as Him glorified and seated at the right hand of Father God. After our surrender to Him, let us see Him in His resurrected, glorified position, as we go about doing good. He is seated at the right hand of the Father on high and so are we. In my first book *Like Him*, I have a whole chapter about this subject which is part of living a resurrected life in Christ Jesus. There is a time to focus on His death and we thank and praise Him for His incredible love for us all. There is also a time to focus on His resurrection heavenly authority, for us, and within us; this enables us to destroy the works of our enemy on earth, as it is in heaven.

Referring back to Luke 24, the women at the tomb saw angels where the body of the Lord had lain. They heard the words of the messengers relate the truth of the matter: 'Why are you seeking the living with the dead: He is not here but He has risen…remember' (Luke 24:5–6). At times, we forget what the Lord God has spoken to us in the past; the prayers, promises, prophecies and the glorious words He has given us personally from His Word. For instance, I referred back to some of my journals recently and found that in July 2017, I wrote a seemingly impossible prayer asking Father God to grant our family a small spa retreat. My husband and I were not remotely thinking of moving premises; however, it was a desire in my heart in order to reach out to others to bless them, as well as enjoying the facilities ourselves. Today I can testify that Father God has granted my request in a wonderful way. Our family now live in a beautiful premises with a mini spa and accommodation attached to it with room to grow. My heart is to share this space with those needing respite, which has begun in some measure.

Ask God, through His Holy Spirit, to remind you of His promises, His prayers, His heart-felt words to you. Thank Him for fulfilling those amazing words in your life. Surely, the Lord will complete the good work He has already begun.[49] Thank You, Lord, for Your wonderful works!

We can focus on Him today and seek Him and His will on earth as in heavenly realms, where He is seated at the right hand of the Father. It is due to the cross and resurrection that we are now spiritually seated with Him. Let us ask for eyes to see what the Father's will is for us today to accomplish on earth as it is in heaven.

Perhaps you have not yet heard God speak with you personally? Let's be encouraged to ask Him and wait patiently for His reply, for He is speaking. He may speak through His Word or in your heart or in various other ways. Wait and listen. He loves to speak to you personally and His Words can change your life forever for the better.

Prayer

Thank You, Holy Spirit, for giving us Your Word and revealing Father God's promises to us.

Thank You for reminding us of the powerful and kind words You have given us Lord Jesus throughout our lives.

Thank You for all that You have done and for Your resurrection power in each one of us, which we can share with others.

Help us to be continually reminded of Your great love and power, and that we are Your priests and kings, we are Your servants, Your disciples, Your children, Your family and together we are Your beautiful Bride.

---

49. Philippians 1:6.

I wait on You, Lord, my delight.
Speak to me personally now, Lord, about today.
Amen.

Resurrection testimony

A man who is seeking after God's will continually is Alexandru
Lourdan. I asked if he had a testimony concerning raising
the dead and this was his answer:[50]

As I was working in a local hospital, my job was to
polish floors with the machine. I passed by the room
of a person who was dying. I heard the doctors and
nurses saying that there was nothing they could do,
they tried 'everything'. I quickly ran into the room . . .
and looked, and the person was cold and stiff. I laid
hands on this person and said: 'Lord, I've seen cancers,
tumours being healed, there is nothing impossible for
You: raise this person up in Jesus' name!'

Nothing happened right away that instant. However,
the next day when I showed up to work, doctors and
nurses were running all over the ward, everybody was
in shock! I tried to find out what was happening, why
all the commotion, so I asked a nurse, she replied that
the person I had prayed for had come back to life and
that was impossible . . .

I came close to the room where the person was, and
they were up and singing and full of joy. That was one
of the best days of my life. There is nothing impossible
for our Lord Jesus Christ!

---

50. Alexandru Lourdan, testimony, 2021. Edited for the purposes of this book.

Another powerful, verifiable testimony which occurred in hospital, this time in Kalgoorlie Hospital in Australia, occurred in Dr Sean George's life. This is the summary:

On October 24, 2008, Sean George, head of general medicine, suffered a fatal heart attack. He was in cardiac arrest for an hour and twenty-five minutes and flatlined for 37 minutes. His wife, also a doctor, arrived and silently prayed for him, to God, for a miracle and suddenly, Sean's heart restarted. His recovery astounded the staff, who had known of his being clinically dead for so long. After undergoing an operation to clear a blocked artery, he completely recovered, returning to his medical practice, and believes that he is alive due to an amazing miracle of God.[51]

---

51. Keener, 'Real Raisings from the Dead or Fake News?'. Permission given by Dr Keener to paraphrase his words, see www.christianitytoday.com/ct/2019/june/miracles-resurrections-real-raisings-fake-news-keener-afric.html (accessed 10.11.22). Please find verification evidence at: https://seangeorge.com.au/ (accessed 25.1.24; permission granted).

8

Peter Raises the Dead

Death was swallowed up in victory.
(1 Corinthians 15:54; from Isaiah 25:8)

The disciples of Jesus raised the dead. This also is a wonderful encouragement to us that we can do the same, as His 'end of days disciples.'

The miracles in the Acts of the apostles tell of a number of people who are raised from the dead. Jesus had died, risen and ascended and the disciples had been commissioned to 'Heal the sick, cleanse the lepers, raise the dead' (Matthew 10:8, NKJV). I believe in these darkening days we are called to do the same. If you feel weak, know that the Lord is strong and it is He who heals the sicknesses, cleanses and raises the dead, by His Holy Spirit within you. Thank the Lord in faith for His boldness and courage as you step out and obey His words and ways.

Through the power of God, Peter raised up a lady called Tabitha (or 'Dorcas' in Greek, which means 'Gazelle'). She was a woman who did many acts of lovingkindness and 'good deeds' continually. I believe the text in Acts 9 mentions the meaning of her name twice, to encourage us, as it shows that she is one who 'skips over mountains' of life 'as swift as the gazelles on the mountains,' 1 Chronicles

12:8, NASB). She was an overcomer who was able to flee the 'enemy lion,' spiritually speaking. She later died in Joppa near the place where Peter happened to be at the time.

Like Jesus, who healed Jairus' daughter, Peter sent the traditional mourners out of the room where Tabitha lay. He knelt down, turned to her body and said: 'Tabitha, you must immediately get up [or arise]. (Acts 9:40) She got up and 'many believed in the Lord' (v. 42).'

Thank the Lord for the 'rock' (Matthew 16:18) Peter was, and that our Lord Jesus is 'The Rock of our salvation' (Psalm 95:1)! I learned more about the apostle Peter, whose journey came 'to life' when I lived in Israel. I was eighteen when I volunteered for seven months in Joppa, Israel, where Peter stayed for some time. I visited the house which the Armenian Church, purported to be Simon the Tanner's house, and went up onto the roof just as Peter had done all those years ago when he had a vision from God. It was this vision in Acts 10 which encouraged Peter to share the good news to non-Jews of Jesus' death, resurrection, and His being the long-awaited Anointed One. Simon the Tanner's house in Joppa (or Jaffa, as it is known nowadays), was once a lighthouse. I remember thinking that this was a fitting place for God to show Peter that Gentiles would thereafter be accepted into the fold. That Jesus was also 'The Light of the world' to Gentiles (John 8:12), and that they too would be enabled to choose to become a light to shine the good news of Jesus' death and resurrection themselves.

I hope you are getting more and more bolstered up in your faith by the resurrection testimonies in each chapter. Here follows another wonderful resurrection testimony.

Resurrection testimony

Pastor Rod Lewis shares in his own words:[52]

In May 2000, my team and I had been invited to a fellowship in Cornwall. I spoke about 'Resurrection Lifestyle' and we all experienced the presence of God's glory there. The following day, after lunch we went for a drive. We parked on the side of the road and were about to set out for a walk, when my team called me over. They had found a man collapsed on a grass verge. He was lifeless. One of our team was a nurse and began CPR and we rang for an ambulance. Sadly, the CPR did not seem to have an effect. 'Let's lay hands on him and pray,' I said to the team. A recent believer repeated the word 'Jesus, Jesus, Jesus' quietly again and again. Meanwhile, I had a burst of faith and said to the man: 'In Jesus' name, come back into your body and be completely healed!' After a few moments he took a gasp of breath; he came back to life before our eyes. The ambulance arrived and took him to hospital and by the next day he was completely well. They had found nothing wrong with his heart. God had shown His power by signs and wonders! To God be the glory for He has done wonderful works!

---

52. Rod Lewis, used with permission. Edited for the purposes of this book. Rod's testimony can be viewed at drrichardkent.org/near-death-experiences/ dr-richard-kent-interviews-rod-lewis-about-his-nde-of-heaven/ (accessed 22.1.24).

9

Abraham and Resurrection

—————◆—————

Ask for faith,
From your Father God,
Who loves to give;
Fruit from the Spirit
Faith and fullness:
A wholesome life.

Biblical narrative is the main source to consider when researching, contemplating and considering resurrection. In the next couple of chapters, we explore some of the Old Testament characters and resurrection.

Abraham had so much faith that he was able to obey God in taking his own son, whom God had promised to him, and offer him as a sacrifice by fire. In Abraham's day, child sacrifice was an acceptable cultural practice, so the act itself would have been known and perhaps, unfortunately, even commonplace. Still, it must have been an extraordinarily difficult journey and action to take, as Isaac was God's promise to 'the father of all nations' (which is the meaning of the name 'Abraham'). Abraham had firm faith that the Lord God could raise Isaac up from the dead: 'He considered that God is able to raise people even from the dead' (Hebrews 11:19, NASB). This is the main reason,

I believe, Abraham went through with God's instruction. God had said it, so it *must* be.

Abraham trusted God with his son's life. After leaving his servants to go to the mountain to offer up Isaac, Abraham even said to his servants, talking of himself and Isaac, that they would both return (Genesis 22:5); Abraham's faith was so strong, he spoke out that which he believed. It is this kind of humble and declaring faith which your God, our God, my God, requires.

In many places in the Bible, it is indicated that God is willing to heal and bring back to life. For example, the leper in Mark 1:41, and Mark 3:10, where Jesus 'healed many,' and in Luke 7:14–15, in which the dead boy was raised to life at his own funeral.

Let us pause for a moment and think about this huge Abrahamic faith. A faith so sure. A faith based on a trusted relationship with God Almighty, that He will do what He says. Even if the fleshly mind, body and soul find it difficult to see and believe and others may judge harshly. It is a faith based on the Word, the instructions and teachings, the ability and character of God, who is a God of love and power. We can question the Lord's instructions to us, but the best and right thing to do is simply believe He is good, that He is a loving God and has the best outcome in mind and to obey Him. We know that it is His voice because it will line up with His character and words portrayed in His Word. If we are not sure it is Him talking to us, we can test the word. Gideon is one in the Bible who did just that by placing a fleece out to test the word he was given, as we see in Judges 6.

It is 'through . . . faith in the working of God' (Colossians 2:12), I would put it to you, which causes each of us to overcome and be an overcomer and to grow in our Jesus

Christ–centred faith. Faith grows, and knowing the heart of Father God, we can trust Him entirely to fix anything and everything because He made everything and everyone. It is a childlike relationship with Father God in faith.

Our Father gave His creation over to us to have dominion in the first place when He made the earth.[53] We are the ones enabled to take initiative, to have faith in Him, even for Him to raise the dead. The Lord knows the beginning and the end, He knows *your* story. He has divine knowledge of your circumstance before it happens. You can have faith that He loves you and has your best interest at heart. He has faith in you. Have you surrendered your whole life and put your entire faith in Him? He will not test you beyond that which you can take.

The relationship between Abraham and Father God was deep and strong; it was said of him that He was 'the Friend of God' (James 2:23, KJV). He was tested and was victorious with the most difficult test of all, to lay down his only son. Abraham passed this great test, and he was given a ram to offer on the altar instead of his son. God supplies all our needs. Father God gave His only Son, Jesus, The Anointed One, as a sacrifice to die on a cross. He was raised up so that you and I can receive His righteousness and a loving, faith filled relationship with Jesus and Father God.

I believe this deep relationship with God our Father, Jesus and Holy Spirit enables us to receive this incredible Abrahamic–like godly faith as we put our trust fully in Him. 'Love the LORD your God with all your . . . might . . .' (Deuteronomy 6:5; see Mark 12:30) is one of the first commands the Lord gives us. Faith is a gift from God,

---

53. 'We will make mankind in our own image . . . [to] have dominion over . . . all the earth' (Genesis 1:26).

and you can ask for more faith for every day and in every circumstance. The Lord has a gift of faith to give to you. If your earthly Father gives you a good gift, how much more will your heavenly Father?[54] We are all called to walk by faith in His Spirit. Live and walk by the Spirit of God.[55]

Prayer

Dear Father God,
Thank You that You are very good.
Thank You for sending your only Son to die and rise for me.
Thank You for growing my faith in You, Lord God,
And making me more like Your Son in word,
In spirit, in truth and in deed.
Amen.

Resurrection testimonies

In current times there are ministers of God, with great faith and authority, who have experienced and have eyewitness verification of the dead being raised up. One aspect of their lives which shines out is their huge faith in our Father God, the God of Abraham, Isaac and Jacob, who does the impossible all the time. These men and women of God are filled with faith and are led by the Spirit on a daily basis; they live dependent on the Mighty God they serve.

Dr Heidi Baker, well known in Christian circles as having raised up sons and daughters who have witnessed and heard first-hand about resurrections from the dead, writes in her blog in 2006 which is found in her book *There is Always Enough*:

54. Luke 11:13
55. Galatians 5:25

During church service people gave their testimonies . . . the next lady had an even more amazing story:

Her husband . . . continued to drink and fly into crazy rages . . . After [this] he was pronounced dead at the hospital, his wife began to pray in Jesus' name. In a little over an hour he was raised from the dead – and came straight to the church to ask Jesus into his heart!

At the same time, he was set free from the demons who had tormented him for years.

This morning he announced with a huge smile that he has not had a drink of alcohol since that day.[56]

CBN media writes about Dr Heidi Baker:

Heidi has watched paralytics walk for the first time after they received prayer. And indigenous pastors, the Bakers trained in Mozambique, have raised 53 people from the dead so far.[57]

During a conference in late 2023 in Israel, I heard Heidi teaching that the key to authority is God's love, and that there is no authority in God without it; so that with the love of God comes the authority of God.[58] In order to raise the dead, we need to be full of God's love, even for our enemies. God's lovingkindness and great faith in Him are two of the main ingredients of resurrection life.

Another person of great authority in God, in our times, who has seen multiple raising from the dead is David

56. Heidi Baker, *There is Always Enough* (Tonbridge: Sovereign World, 2003).
57. 'Heidi Baker's Uncomfortable Message to America', www.CBN.com, www2.cbn.com/article/sin/heidi-bakers-uncomfortable-message-america (accessed 10.12.22).
58. Holy Convocation, Jerusalem House of Prayer for All Nations, Yom Kippur 2023.

Hogan. His website gives many testimonies of people, showing photographs of each:

> This lady was pregnant when a plague came through her village. She got sick and the baby died in her womb and after being hiked out of her village on her way to the city she also died. Fourteen hours later she and the baby were raised from the dead in the morgue after her death certificate had already been made out.

> This lady and her family were not saved and then she died. The people from the town came by to pay their respects, along with them came two pastors. They prayed for her, and God raised her from the dead. She and her family then came to Jesus.[59]

Reinhard Bonnke was another incredible man of authority in God, who was a testimony of a missionary evangelist's life set apart to God. The following is an interview with Pat Robertson of CBN *700 Club,* of a man raised from the dead as a result of one of Reinhard's Christ for All Nations Nigerian crusades:

> 'BONNKE: We see testimonies like this man coming back to life.

> ROBERTSON: I want you to tell us about him. He was in one of your meetings. He was hit by a car. I understand he was stiff and rigormortis had set in. I don't know if they had embalmed him or not.

59.   David Hogan, www.freedom-ministries.us (2022 testimonies, accessed 12.12.22).

BONNKE: They did.

ROBERTSON: He had been embalmed?

BONNKE: He was embalmed, but not the way it is done in America with the removal of organs. They injected chemicals into the body to slow down decay, since there was no refrigeration.

ROBERTSON: So what happened?

BONNKE: His wife was one with a promise from God; that woman ... received back the dead by resurrection. She said, 'My husband will come back, and I have heard Reinhard Bonnke is in Onitsha this Sunday I will bring him there.' She brought him there. I was preaching and I knew nothing about it. Suddenly, the man started to breathe. His story is awesome.'[60]

Thank the Lord for great men and women of God today and in the past who have great faith and are doing exploits in the name of Jesus our Lord, through His Spirit, might, love and power.

---

60. Reinhard Bonnke Tells of Nigerian Man Raised from the Dead, CBN, www2. cbn.com/article/salvation/reinhard-bonnke-tells-nigerian-man-raised-dead (accessed 16.1.24).

10

Elisha and Resurrection

Having death under our feet
enables us,
to defeat the devil
in all his ways.

Elisha, one of the great Old Testament prophets, experienced the Almighty God's resurrection power. And in 2 Kings 4:32 we read of the Shunamite's son coming back to life after a kind of brain aneurism or similar, during the reaping of the harvest that year: 'And he said to his father, My head. My head!...he sat on [his mother's] knees till noon then died.' (2 Kings 4:19–20).

The story did not end here, however. Even though her son lay completely dead in a room in her home, the Shunamite had great faith pronouncing: 'It is well' in verse 23 and then again, 'It is well,' (verse 26), when she met the prophet's servant. This reminds us of the famous hymn: 'It is Well'.[61] When we have God with us, our souls can rest in the knowledge that He will restore that which has been lost. You and I can be enabled to sing and say 'It is Well' in faith, full of the strength of the Lord God even in a time

---

61. Horatio Spafford (1828–88), 'It is Well', www.hymnal.net/en/hymn/h/341 (accessed 16.1.24).

of turbulence. We can sing or say in faith and the Lord's delight will come to be in us, to bring transformation and resurrection life! Whatever the situation, speak out, or sing out God's word in faith. Praise and worship help lift us and help us focus our eyes on God, especially in difficult circumstances.

The Shunamite had great faith stating that it was well with her son. She had faith that God had promised her this boy through Elisha the prophet, and therefore may have felt that the Lord would not allow him an early death; the son was a gift from God through Elisha's prophetic words to her.

The narrative continues as Gehazi, Elisha's servant, runs ahead of Elisha and endeavours to raise the boy from the dead by placing Elisha's staff over his face, to no avail. Elisha then shuts himself in the room with the boy, prays, and lies on top of him. It is written that he 'put his mouth to his mouth, eyes upon his eyes and his hands upon his hands.' It is written that the boy's flesh then 'waxed warm' (2 Kings 4:34). Elisha walked to and fro in the house after this, returning to the boys' bedside and stretching himself on the boy a second time; upon which the boy, 'sneezed seven times' (v. 35) and then opened up his eyes!

Why and how was the boy raised from the death? It was due to a number of factors: the Shunamite's faith, Elisha's obedience to the Lord, by lying on him, then being face to face with the boy – we assume, instructed by God himself. Perhaps it was also the Shunamite's tenacity in seeking after God's blessing through His prophet?

The meaning for the word 'resurrection' is 'rising up from lying down'. Elisha lay down on the boy and then he rose up and walked to and fro, in a type of prophetic actioning. Perhaps he 'rose up' off the boy in faith, being encouraged that the boy began to 'wax warm'.

It is interesting that primarily Gehazi placed Elisha's staff over the boy's face as instructed by Elisha. When nothing occurred, Elisha then put his own face over the boy's. In Scripture there are many instances of the Lord God being 'face to face' with humankind. For example, Genesis 32:31, it is written: Jacob called the name of the place Peniel: 'For I have seen God face to face and my life is preserved.' Elisha's name means: 'God is my salvation,' and so here we see a picture in the text of 'God is my salvation', face to face with the dead boy. The name of 'Yeshua,' or Jesus, means 'salvation.' I put it to you that there is a hyperlink to the resurrection power of Jesus Himself at work here. I am reminded of John 1: '. . . and the Word was God . . . the Word became flesh and lived among us.' Jesus' Holy Spirit is inside you and I, and we are a dwelling place for His love and resurrection power.

Throughout the whole of Scripture, we see the resurrection power of Jesus, the very Word of God at work. What an action–packed resurrected life of wonder!

The action of Elisha lying down on the boy, is also a prophetic picture of Jesus laying down His life for us so that we can be restored to life; so that we can live a resurrected life.

The Shunamite had faith in Elisha's relationship with God and is described as a 'great woman' in 2 Kings 4:8, perhaps she was called great also because of her great faith in God. She knew to go as fast as she could to fetch Elisha when the boy died.

Have great faith in Jesus, who is your salvation, who laid down His life for you, that you may have resurrection life in your body, mind and spirit daily. You can run to Him when you face all kinds of difficulty and even when you face death itself.

Laying down to rise up

Here is another perspective which runs continually through scripture: we, like Jesus, can willingly lay our lives down for others to relieve their suffering. We may not need to lie down on a dead person like Elisha, however, the Lord God may lead us to give sacrificial love by laying down our lives for others in other ways. Let us simply obey the instructions our God gives to us.

> I urge, you brothers, through the compassion of God, to present your bodies holy, living offerings, pleasing to God, your spiritual service...
>
> *(Romans 12:1)*

For example, during a season of my life, I mentored two young mothers who needed a mature, stable input. One of the very young mothers had an abusive ex-partner. There was a time when I met him face to face during a random visit, putting my own life at risk. I was informed that he had a knife and had used it in the past. It was important that the young lady could see that I was not intimidated by her ex-partner. I acted as a role model and overcame any fear. I felt safe due to my faith in God rather than any human strength. Just me being with her enabled her to gain more strength for her and her child. Being with this young lady was a kind of willingly laying down of my own life to support hers. I still pray for her today.

In the same fashion, others have also sacrificed their time and energy to encourage and support my life. We need each other, and can show the sacrificial love of Jesus, from which flows His resurrection life.

The kind Shunamite

In 2 Kings 8, we find a continuation of the Shunamite's story where Elisha warns her of a seven-year famine in the land. She travels to safety for those years and returns to find her land taken over. When she goes to request the land back from the king, Gehazi, Elisha's understudy, just so happens to be relating the testimony of Elisha resurrecting her son. The king, perhaps seeing that she had been greatly blessed by the prophet and by God, orders her lands to be reinstated by armed guard.

When we relate any testimony of resurrection, such as the Gehazi and Shunamite did, God works in marvellous ways, and the testimony brings hope, faith and favour, where there once was none. This is one reason I wanted to write this book. Resurrection testimonies are powerful and show divine intervention, which in turn brings great favour, even from kings, in the Shunamite's case.

Giving testimony of healing, miracles and resurrection life, opens up doors of blessing, doors of restoration and destroys the works of the enemy. In the text, the Shunamite was able to go and rebuild her life where she left off, and she was greatly blessed.

There is a hidden lesson in this story. The Shunamite's acts of lovingkindness and hospitality to God's favoured prophet, 'God is salvation,' is seen by God, and thereafter reward and favour follow. We find this hospitable favour with other great ladies of the Bible, including Rebekah (Genesis 24) and, in the New Testament, the woman at the well (John 4). Rebecca brought gallons of water to thirsty camels (each camel may have drunk twenty gallons!) The woman at the well gave a drink to the Messiah when he thirsted in John 4. Acts of lovingkindness are important to Father God. It may be argued that the servant heart of these great women led to a prosperous life in the spiritual as well as the natural.

Rebekah is remembered as one of the matriarchs of Israel, and the woman at the well spread the spiritual living water of the Words of the Lord far and wide.

This kind of lovingkindness is a characteristic of 'The Bride of Messiah.' Attributes of sacrificial giving to others; we are and will be, rewarded for our acts of lovingkindness. Like the Shunamite, who experienced God's resurrection life for her son, the woman at the well experienced restoration of her life when she met Jesus, her Messiah, and gave testimony. Jesus accepted her and caused a woman, living an unhealthy lifestyle, to be whole and full of His joy; to be able to share about Jesus, Messiah with the entire town.

Resurrection testimony

During 2019 and 2020, I attended an excellent mission school which enabled me to grow further in confidence in sharing my faith with others. During this time, I heard that Jonathan Conrathe, the senior leader, had seen God raise people from the dead. Following is one of those testimonies.

The preacher, teacher and evangelist Jonathan Conrathe, whom I met while on the impactful Mission24 Mission Course, gave us personal testimony of one of five supernatural back–to–life experiences he has witnessed in his lifetime, so far, during his mission work. The following are notes taken from Jonathan's teaching on Resurrection of the Dead:[62]

---

62. Jonathan Conrathe, Mission24 senior leader and evangelist. Resurrection testimony 2022 teaching, word of mouth, written by author. Edited for the purposes of this book.

Jonathan told us of a lady who was raised from the dead in Mityama, Uganda. The background to the story is that Jonathan was praying about this upcoming mission and believed that he heard from the Lord the words: 'Why do you think it a strange thing that God should raise the dead?' Thereafter, he had a 'knowing' that someone would be raised from the dead during this particular mission. One evening, the team was at a meeting of around 5,000 local people where God, by His Holy Spirit, was doing supernatural signs and wonders: the lame were healed, deaf could hear and the blind could see!

During the ministry time, suddenly the crowd split into two, to create a pathway to bring a dead woman down for prayer. Jonathan and his brother stepped over to pray. They checked her pulse – no pulse, the lady was not breathing, her eyes were rolled up into her head and her skin dark blue/black. Jon and his brother agreed that they were to pray for her to be raised from the dead. Jon rebuked the spirit of death 'in Jesus' name!' And commanded her spirit to come back into her body. After a few of minutes of these strong prayers and declarations, the woman gasped deeply for air and colour came back to life. She patted her stomach, looking around in bewilderment. She explained to the translator that she had had several stomach tumours which the doctors had indicated would cause imminent death. She had gone to the gospel mission in faith, but during the meeting she had collapsed. Immediately after this, she saw Jesus in a powerful way, full of glorious light. The next thing she remembers was hearing Jonathan's voice saying: 'Receive life in Jesus' name!' At the same moment, there was a beautiful wind that came out from Jesus and into her. It was at this moment that she could take a breath once more.

Jonathan marvelled that people who are in another realm can hear our voices in prayer when we declare life over them. The lady was completely healed of the several cancer tumours, as well as raised back to life in Jesus' name! Many people came to the Lord in the locality through this lady's testimony as she shared about how Jesus gave her life back to her and healed all of her disease. Thanks be to God!

11

Elijah and Resurrection

———◆———

Whom you were also raised
through your faith in the working of God,
The One Who raised Him
from *the company of the* dead …
(Colossians 2:12)

The spiritual 'father' of the great prophet Elisha was Elijah. In Scripture we find another wonderful testimony of the son of a widowed woman who was raised back to life. Like the Shunamite woman, she also was greatly hospitable to the prophet, who received resurrection power from God.

And he said to her, Give me your son . . . and carried him up into a loft where he stayed, and laid him on his own bed. And he cried to the LORD and said, LORD my God, have You also brought evils upon the widow with whom I am staying by slaying her son? And he stretched himself upon the child three times and cried to the LORD, and said, 'LORD my God, I pray you, let this child's life come into him again.' And the LORD heard the voice of Elijah and the life of the child came into him again and he revived.
(1 Kings 17:19)

We see in the text that Elijah's voice was heard by the Lord, and the Lord answered him. It would seem that those who dying, who are 'crossing over,' can hear our voices from earth, as we pray for them. You can have faith that the spiritual unseen world can hear your voice as you declare statements in line with the words of God and according to His promises. For instance, we can have faith and speak out that Jesus is willing and able to cleanse and heal us. The leper declared to Jesus: 'You are able to cleanse me.' Jesus replied: 'I am willing, you must immediately be cleansed: and the leprosy left him at once.' (Luke 5:12–13)

The faith which we have in our hearts is powerful, and even more so as we vocalise the faith we have. In Genesis 1:3, God said: '"Let there be light," and there was light' (ESV). God spoke out to bring things into being from the heavens to the earth. Remember, Jesus' Spirit is in us and: '. . . if the Spirit of the One Who raised Y'shua [Jesus] from the dead dwells in you, the One who raised Messiah . . . will also make [you] alive . . . because He abides within you.' (Romans 8:11)

We find a similar testimony to the widows in the New Testament, after Jesus has died and had risen. Paul prays for a boy who had been listening to his sermon. Eutychus was getting very tired and weary, and the hour was late. Paul had the ability to talk for many hours and Eutychus fell completely asleep, unfortunately falling out of the window. We read in Acts 20:10: 'Paul went down, threw himself on the young man and put his arms around him. "Don't be alarmed," he said. "He's alive!"'

Paul did not say a prayer over the young man, he simply embraced him. In a similar way, Elijah connected with the dead boy by lying upon him in 1 Kings 17:18–24. We also learned that this is how Elisha raised the dead back to life in 2 Kings 4. This contact with the dead bodies would have made the two prophets and Apostle Paul ritually unclean, according to Levitical instruction, and so they would have needed to take a *mikvah* (ritual baptism) after raising these people from the dead and then confine themselves for some time. At times, the Lord God requires us to do things which seems ritually and traditionally 'out of the box'. The actions of the Old Testament prophets were 'messianic' in essence, meaning that they were a foreshadowing of that which was to come: the coming of the Messiah Himself, Jesus Christ, who would raise up others and be raised Himself.

I believe, that living a loving, laid-down life; walking by the Spirit of God, walking like Jesus, being like Him; increases the probability of seeing a life once dead, then raised from the dead. What a good motivation for living a godly life.

Resurrection testimony

Paula O'Keefe is one of my oldest and dear friends, has led the laid-down life of a missionary all her life. Here she shares a testimony in her own words:[63]

It was the summer of 2001 and we were at the glorious Black Sea in Southern Russia hosting a camp for refugees from Chechnya, Russia. One of the campers Alan ... was so thrilled to be away from the war and his ... dream was to learn to swim.

At the camp, he shared a dormitory with Kevin ... When Kevin found out Alan couldn't swim, he promised

63. Reprinted by permission. "Miracles in the Midst of War", Paula O'Keefe, 23 January 2024, Sovereign World Ltd, Lancaster, England. All Rights Reserved.

to teach him. 'I'll give you my goggles if you learn to swim,' he said.

One night Kevin awoke to see Alan sneaking into the room, seemingly drunk. He staggered onto his bed, threw up, then passed out. When Kevin examined him, however, he realised it was serious . . .

'Something's terribly wrong with Alan. Come quickly, I thought he was drunk, but I'm not sure. He's in a bad way.'

Dashing into the boys' dorm, I took one look at Alan and gasped. His eyes had rolled up into the back of his head, and he was turning blue. 'Jesus, You have to help us here, I can't have Kheda lose another family member, not after losing her husband . . .' I prayed inwardly.

We prayed for him. No response. None at all . . . Suddenly, gentle little Margaret spoke with an incredible authority that must have made all the demons in the area stand to attention: 'I bind you, spirit of death, in the name of Jesus, and I speak life into you, Alan, right now.' Alan's eyes popped open as the words left her mouth. Looking straight at me and then at Margaret, he reassured us: 'Don't worry, I'll be alright now.' With that, he turned over and went to sleep, as if nothing had happened.

'Amazing!' we whispered excitedly to each other . . . In the morning, Alan was as bright as a button as he explained what had happened: '. . . I decided to go and practice my swimming. I waited until everyone had gone to bed and crept out and tried to go swimming in the sea. Suddenly out of nowhere this big wave came over me, dragging me under the water, and I couldn't seem to find the surface, swallowing loads of water.

I nearly drowned. I was really petrified. I prayed and somehow got back onto the land. I lay on the beach for a while. I have no idea how I managed to crawl back to our dorm room.' He'd swallowed large amounts of sea water, some of which had accumulated in his lungs, causing him to stop breathing (known as 'secondary drowning'). But God had healed him and raised him.

12

Arise and Shine, Church of the Lord!

———◆———

Arise, and give Light! For your Light has come, and the
Glory of the LORD has shone like the sun upon you.

(Isaiah 60:1)

One of the central aspects of the resurrected life is to know
that we are all joined together as 'the Bride of Messiah,'
by the Holy Spirit. The resurrected life is to know we are
betrothed to our Messiah Jesus; we belong to Him and
He belongs to us. To walk together as His Bride, His body,
His *Ekklesia*, is at the core of our identity individually and
corporately.

Who is this arising Bride-to-be of the Lamb of God in the
earth? Is she corporately and individually the faithful ones
who have received the Lamb's name, who have received
His Spirit and Word; who have shone, glorifying Our Father
with their good works of lovingkindness?[64] Are some of
those good works raising the dead? We can say, 'Yes
and Amen.'

The Bible has many metaphors; one of the most
powerful is that of the spiritual, corporate picture of the
Bride-to-be of the Messiah Jesus. Many believe that this
spiritual image and story of 'the Bride of the Messiah,'

---

64. Matthew 5:16.

is dramatically and song-fully detailed in the book of the: 'Song of Songs', which uses intimate language to portray their personal relationship. The story or 'Song' is shared with the inhabitants of the City of Peace, and the villages surrounding ('daughters of Jerusalem', and 'My companions,' NASB, 8:13) between a king (Solomon) and a beautiful shepherdess (Shulamite/Shunamite,) who represents the Bride of Jesus Messiah. In the poem, the lover-king goes to the bride-to-be's house and knocks at her door; he asks her to arise from her bed; she does not arise, as she is comfortably in bed and has prepared herself to slumber. Towards the end of the poem, however, she realises, awakens and changes her mind, dramatically declaring: 'Let's spend the night in the villages. Let's rise early.' (Song of Songs 7:11-12, NASB)

The bride-to-be is captivated and wooed by the King's love for her, and she eventually realises the depth of her love for him, and together they rise early in the morning. This is a beautiful image of the corporate Bride of Messiah becoming closer than close, and arising together with her Lord to go out into the dark places. The fruits of this deep love between them affect more than just the Bride and Groom-to-be. The 'villages,' a whole 'City of Peace,' called Jerusalem, and the kingdom are affected by the love of the King and His shepherdess Bride. New life is created in the natural through supernatural intimacy with our Bridegroom-to-be. Our Messiah Jesus creates resurrection new life; this not only affects each of us personally, but this faithful love of God also spills out of us into the world as we, the betrothed Church of Jesus, 'shine' His heavenly light of life within us into the darkness of death itself.

There is a sense that the western Church, as the Bride of the Messiah has, on the whole, in the past decades, been spiritually asleep to much of the 'greater works.' (John 14:12, ESV) The Lord Jesus, her betrothed Beloved, is calling out and waking her up to do these greater works. Many are saying that now is the time of our awakening, for our Lord has poured out His love upon us.

How does this metaphor of the Bride of Messiah, which is the Church, manifest on earth? Is it in the deep and loving worship of a whole congregation to the Lord God? Is it glimpsed in the healing miracle of the disabled, blind or deaf through the prayer of God's ministers? Is it heard through the faithful and heartfelt prayer of those in love with His beauty and in need of His love? All of these, as well as one of the more neglected acts of lovingkindness of our King of power and love: the resurrection of one who was once dead but is now come back to life (at least in the western Church this could be said to have been the neglected case in the past). Let you and I, 'The Bride', arise and receive boldness and courage from our Bridegroom King, to do the works He asked of us.

One of the main aspects the Bride of Messiah needs to know, is her *identity*, who she is, and her place in Messiah's kingdom. She needs to know this both individually and corporately. She is seated in heavenly places with Jesus who has subjected all authorities under His feet.[65] She is a priest and royalty to serve Him, her beloved betrothed High Priest and King. We can learn about how to be a priest to serve our Lord, as we gather in our churches. Our local church, Living Word, is teaching on this very subject presently, which is a great encouragement.

Individually, we are crucified with Messiah and raised to life with Him through salvation, repentance, through

---

65. Ephesians 2:6, Ephesians 1:22.

baptism in His name, by the water of His Word and by His Holy Spirit. I wrote a short poem while contemplating this, (Galatians 2:20) inspired by HIs Word and Spirit:

Raised Up

Crucified with Him
No longer do I live.
Christ lives in me.
The life I live.
I live by faith.
In the Son of God
The One who loves me.
Seated with Him
At His right hand
Above all power
In the heavens,
On the earth
And under the earth.
I must have faith.
In all that He is,
And in all that I am.
He is the I AM
Who raises the dead,
He has raised me
Spiritually.

The above is true corporately, for the whole Bride of Christ, the whole Church. We need to listen, to see, that which our Father is doing, just like Jesus does; we need to be at one and agree with the living Word's main core beliefs. These are: Jesus is Lord; He died and rose again to save humanity; we must be baptised and be filled with His Holy

Spirit and submit to His Word and ways. Can we look to Him and listen together and endeavour to lay aside our secondary differences of interpretation? When we are full of His Spirit and His Word, we are able to do His exploits, such as raising the dead.

You may need to know that you belong, that you are adopted into the family of the Father God. You are also betrothed to your Bridegroom heavenly King. For some weeks now, if not months, I have heard the sweet, and yet strong voice of God Himself in my heart. He says to me quite simply: 'I give you my Troth' and then: 'You are betrothed to me.' Accompanied with this is a strong sense of belonging to the Lord forever. A deep rest and relief are in those words, which anchor me and fill me up with love. Whatever is going on in my day, I know that I have a righteous rest, because my Bridegroom Saviour has a strong forever-love for me which is eternal, the kind of love which never, ever fails. I found the scripture which matches the words I heard over many weeks:

And I will betroth you to Me forever. Yes, I shall betroth you to Me in righteousness and in loving kindness and in compassion . . . I shall even betroth you to Me in faithfulness, and you will know the LORD.

(Hosea 2:21-22)

His Word has literally kept me moving forward, to be at peace. I pray that you also will have a knowledge of His promise to you. That you would know you belong to Jesus, that you have a continual knowledge of Him, your beloved Betrothed. He is your anointed Messiah, and you can trust His words. He has given all that you need to be able to trust, forgive and be forgiven. He has enabled you to repent and turn away from all chaos, evil and unrighteous behaviour, to become His spotless Bride. Together we are His.

Rest

Another aspect of being the Bride of Messiah Jesus, and therefore living the resurrection life, is to know his complete peace and walk continually in His rest. Make God your strength and do not trust in riches, or the ways of humankind. Make an intentional start to the day in prayer and focus on His words in the Bible. Be aware of His love continually in your innermost being as you work and dialogue with others. Lean into His Word and Spirit throughout the day, asking questions if you do not understand, or know what to do with His Words. Speak in the spiritual language He has given you as you go.[66] Do not let stress, nor any other wrong, or bad thing invade the kingdom peace inside your heart and in your mind. I wrote another poem as I meditated on this subject:

Rest
It is an Arising rest,
A moving rest
Without a stress.
A rest from toil,
Resting from affliction
And addiction,
And deception.
From scornful cries,
A rest of no shame.
Freedom from all pain.

---

66. See 1 Corinthians 12:10. Speaking in other languages is a gift of the Holy Spirit.

It is not just a duvet day,
It is The Life, The Truth, His Way.
The Lord says to us:
'Come and rest in me,
Let My kingdom come,
Lay down at my feet,
Come and rest.'

As we begin each day, let us begin in His rest and endeavour to remain in His restful gaze. In Psalm 37, the song encourages us to rest in the Lord and 'wait patiently for Him' (v. 7). It is in the stillness of the presence of His rest, that we can hear His voice. We can receive His words for guidance and walk in a life of faith–filled peace; a life which leads to His arising life in you. It is from this place of rested faith that we can arise and, 'know Him and the power of His resurrection' (Philippians 3:10). In Hebrew, rest means wholeness in life and complete, perfect peace in every area of life: *shalom*. This is the kind of whole and simple life the Lord has promised us, which will affect all those around us as we walk in rest, in perfect peace, in Jesus. Everything is possible in God!

Resurrection life is about entering His rest, His 'promised land,' so to speak. Some Jews and Christians rest on a Saturday *shabbat,* or Sabbath. They rest from their work on the seventh day. The Lord is the 'Lord even of the Sabbath' (Matthew 12:8, NKJV) and wants us to enter His rest. I believe it is when we practise this during the week and at the weekend, we live in resurrection life. We are living a foreshadowing of our eternal promised rest. 'It is now, though, not yet,' my pastor tells me. Then all things will be completely peaceful; there will be no war, disease, blemish, or bad behaviour. A righteous life is an active, restful resurrection life, lived in the present reality in Messiah Jesus. I believe that there is a blessing in keeping the Sabbath rest and taking a complete day of rest. It is written in Genesis 2:3: 'And God blessed the seventh day and sanctified it, because in it He had rested from all His work.' Whether we rest on Saturday or Sunday, or both, this is surely a blessing to us and to Father God. Jesus said: 'The Sabbath was made for man, and not man for the Sabbath' (Mark 2:27). Sunday is the eighth day when Jesus was raised from the dead, hence the reasoning behind why we rest and celebrate on a Sunday as Christians.[67] I write this due to many factions and disagreements about the day of rest to be celebrated. Can we all say together: 'This is the day that the LORD has made; let us rejoice and be glad in it?' (Psalm 118:24, ESV).

Wonder

A central aspect of walking in resurrection life is to live and walk through life with the childlike wonder of God the Father. Jesus walked in this wonder of our Father God when he lived on earth; He saw what the Father was doing in heaven; He listened and obeyed.

Resurrection life is a spontaneous, active living in the present reality of the wonder of Creator and creation. In his

---

67. '...in ancient times, Sunday – which was also known as the first day of the week, was also referred to as the eighth day by Christians.' https://thesacredfaith.co.uk/home/perma/1477516140/article/the-eighth-day.html (accessed 25.1.24).
Other source: Barnabas wrote: '"when resting from all things I shall begin the eighth day, that is, the beginning of the other world." (Isa 1:13; Rev 21:1)' Bar 13:9–10, www.thefirmament.org/wp-content/uploads/pdf/Barnabas.pdf (accessed 25.1.24).
Other relevant scripture: Numbers 29:35: 'On the eighth day you shall have a solemn assembly; you shall do no laborious work' (NASB).

book: *Living the Resurrection: The Risen Christ in Everyday Life*, Eugene Peterson writes about the astonishing willingness to: 'stop what we are doing, to stand still open-eyed, open-handed, ready to take in what is "more and other."'[68] He writes that this wonder is not often present in the workplace. The workplace is where we spend much of our time, if we work for a living.

These resurrection life moments can be seen in the Bible where, for instance, Moses 'turned aside' (see Exodus 3:3) during his work day and he saw a burning bush ... he may have wondered, 'what is happening?' . . . the bush spoke with the voice of the 'I AM' (Exodus 3:14). Moses received the identity of his destiny that day! Let us not forsake turning aside in wonder at work, where it may be more difficult to focus in on listening for God's voice; be aware of His presence with us and in us. Let us intentionally listen to the Holy Spirit's prompting at work and look for His wonder in the work we do.

Jesus, being God, *caused* a wonder; for instance, he was approaching Nain, where He had compassion on the widow's only son, whose funeral procession was being undertaken, as we have learnt earlier. It is written that 'profound awe gripped them all' (Luke 7:16, AMP) as the dead man sat up in his coffin and began to speak! Scripture and modern-day testimony of coming back to life after death, give us hope and encourage us to live a peace-filled, simple lives, full of faith; to expect our miraculous God to manifest His glory through us.

The Holy Spirit filled me one morning and spoke clearly, that when I am full of the fullness of Him, everything I do has the anointing of Messiah Jesus in it. I can do all things

---

68. Eugene H. Peterson, *Living the Resurrection: The Risen Christ in Everyday Life* (Colorado Springs, CO: Navpress, 2006).

to the Lord. I surrender myself to a fleshly death and rise in the glory of His Holy Spirit resurrection life. The very essence of the 'I am' is flowing through our bodies to bring healing and life to our mortal bodies, as well as to those around us. We can impart to others the resurrection life of the Lord through His Holy Spirit. Let us be full of the His glorious, faith and love-filled, resurrection life.[69]

Resurrection testimony

We need to be intentional in our walk, serving and watching for opportunities to release God's power and love. Tracy Bates, a co-alumni with Mission24, the mission school I attended, writes of her personal testimony about two resurrection miracles experienced in the UK on the streets and in the church she attends:

My husband and I were out on a street pastor's shift on a rainy Saturday night. 'On patrol' we came across a distressed young lady and her boyfriend who was very drunk. Taxis were refusing to take them so we brought them to the pastor table to sober up. The boy was slipping in and out of consciousness and we managed to induce vomiting. His pulse was erratic and he was thereafter unresponsive. An ambulance was called but the ETA was forty to sixty minutes. My husband was holding him upright in a chair, while I monitored his breathing and pulse along with another Street Pastor. The other helper declared, 'He's gone!' I checked for a pulse and there was no pulse; his heart had stopped and he had started to turn blue. As a paramedic-

---

69. 'And God was doing extraordinary miracles by the hands of Paul, so that even handkerchiefs or aprons that had touched his skin were carried away to the sick, and their diseases left them' (Acts 19:11-12, ESV).

trained first-aider, my first response should have been CPR. But instead, I found myself declaring, 'Oh no, you are not dying on my watch! Death I rebuke you! In Jesus' name, come back!' The young man gasped and suddenly his heart started beating; his colour returned. The ambulance arrived.

We never saw him again; but heard later that he survived. He was twenty-one years old and that night was the anniversary of his mum's death.

The second testimony is about a young woman who came for the first time to our church, she was heavily pregnant.

She was quietly sobbing throughout the service. I asked her what had brought her there that morning, and could I pray for her and baby. I prayed peace for her so she could find the words to tell me what was wrong. The baby had stopped moving and she had been told he was dead.

She would have to give birth to a dead baby. I remember feeling angry as I prayed for the baby; I could not stand the thought of her having to deliver a dead baby. With great determination I put a hand at baby's head and one at his feet; my hands were red-hot. It felt like a battle. As I prayed and I commanded life into the baby – he gave me an almighty kick! Then he moved his head and his hands! I could feel baby moving under my hands and pressing his head into the palm of my hand as he fluttered his feet. Mum was overwhelmed with joy! Two months later a perfect, beautiful, baby boy was born. That little boy had been resurrected. We serve a mighty God.[70]

70.   Tracy M. Bates, Love Inspire Foundation, 2022. Edited for the purposes of this book.

13

Resurrection Life Every Day

Therefore we have been buried with
Him through baptism into death,
so that, just as Christ was raised from the
dead through the glory of the Father,
so we too may walk in newness of life.

(Romans 6:4, NASB)

Experiencing God's resurrection life in our individual lives changes us for good. One week at church, we had a retreat, when the church building was open for several days and evenings to seek the Lord. On one of the evenings, I went intentionally to worship. We were encouraged to walk around the big auditorium and move, walk and even dance with God. At one point I lay down and found myself in a crucifix position, as led by the Holy Spirit. As I was praying, I felt a huge sense of pain and heaviness; it was like I was being crucified inside, and this had a physical effect on my body. This continued for some time until I was 'fully dead' to my fleshly self. I then moved to a standing position and immediately felt a mighty energy rush, and went into a holy dance before the Lord in the Spirit. It is one of the best and most energetic times of dance to the Lord God I have ever experienced. It was as if I were flying and dancing all at the same time. There was no one to watch, as each person in the retreat was individually praying to God. There was a sense of resurrection life which surged into me, and I was forever changed. I know that God can bring resurrection life to us all, and that this requires the full worship of sacrificial surrender. Smith Wigglesworth spoke of this: 'You must come to a place of whole-hearted surrender ... where you are prepared to be despised by everybody ... He sets you on high because you have known His name (Psalm 91:14)'.[71]

There are resurrection moments in our spiritual journey into a life living for Messiah Jesus. We can experience the baptismal process of dying in Christ and arising into 'newness of life'. As we surrender our lives to Jesus through repentance and acceptance of the promise of His Word and Spirit, we are made righteous by His blood; we will also experience physical resurrection life of heavenly realms when we die.

A glimpse of this was heard when Jesus died on the cross. He cried out: 'It is finished' (John 19:30, ESV). The sun went dark[72] and there was an earthquake,[73] and many who were asleep rose from the dead![74] John's Gospel pointed to this happening when John wrote that: 'a time is coming and even now has arrived, when the dead will hear the voice of the Son of God, and those who hear will live' (John 5:25, NASB).

The voice of the Son of God is still raising the dead. His voice uttered: 'Let there be light' (Genesis 1:3, AMP) and it appeared. The sound of His voice causes creative miracles

---

71. Dr Michael H. Yeager, *God Still Raises the Dead'* (Scotts Valley, CA: CreateSpace Independent Publishing, 2018).
72. Matthew 27:45.
73. Matthew 27:51.
74. Matthew 27:52-53.

to happen, and new life is created. The resurrection power that raised Jesus from the dead is in you. You have the sound of His voice within you. Declare the word of the Lord today! As you surrender and submit to Him, through His amazing grace and mercy; He has chosen you to declare and be a conduit for His resurrection power, peace and love.

Many times, the Lord Jesus simply spoke words such as: 'Be healed' (Mark 5:34, NKJV) or 'take up your bed, and walk' (John 5:8, ESV). His voice is *the voice* of faith itself. Even when we have a small seed of this faith within us, and speak out His words, the whole of heaven is behind His and our words to create newness of life on earth.

The resurrection life here on earth is one of living continually in communion with the Author of resurrection itself: Jesus The Messiah. I believe that resurrection life is a life of active rest. Not rest in the sense of not working, but rest in the sense of being in and with Jesus and knowing that you can be free from sin, death and hell; that you are destined for an eternal perfect rest. It is a rest in faith, that you are covered by the 'blood of the Lamb' and of the 'word of [your] testimony' (Revelation 12:11). A rest in the sealing of your life in His life. A belonging in His family. When a person is promised, betrothed to another, they take on their name, both in recent and ancient times. You and I are adopted into the life of Jesus our Saviour, so that we can know our Father in heaven, whilst on earth. It is a journey into being one with The One who is perfect and holy.

There is an active rising up to do the works of lovingkindness, which are part of the resurrection life in Jesus which we, as the Church, are called to do. Feeding the poor, visiting the sick, loving people physically and financially; as well as praying for them spiritually. Perhaps the beautiful wedding garments of the Bride are these works, which clothe her with lovingkindness, praise and His glory. This is good motivation to be involved daily with His lovingkindness. Go together with those who are in love with Messiah and be His Bride on earth.

Love

Love is the main ingredient of the raised-up lifestyle. When Jesus was raised up, He showed love by teaching truths to His disciples on the Emmaus Road, as we see in Luke 24. And in John 21, He made a special breakfast for some of them and restored Peter, asking him: 'Do you love me?'

His love is like a hallmark on a golden wedding ring of those betrothed to Him, our Bridegroom. It is the mark which causes the world to see who His Bride is. His love causes His Bride to be able to 'hit the mark,' and be His true body on earth. The Lord gave up His earthly life for us and showed us how to love His way. A life of sacrifice, a life of worship to Him, a life submitting to His will, a life of receiving His love; a love which flows out to others.

Faith

Seeds of faith arise in us, as we intentionally focus on doing what is right in God, turning our hearts to Him. The other day I was propagating plants. The soil was bare, and I placed a tiny seed into the pot of compost. It seemed as though nothing was there at all. I looked at all the pots – the compost was 'formless and empty' (see Genesis 1:2, NLT), yet I hovered over it with a watering can and I kept on sprinkling it with refreshing waters. I will keep on sprinkling. A few days later, there was a tiny green plant pushing its way through the earth, which I thought was empty! I knew in my heart it was not empty, as I had placed a seed there – still, each time I am in wonder! Every small plant seems to me like a miracle, as we had come through a hard winter and then it was springtime. It was the time of springing up into 'resurrection life'. An arising life is something God does; we may plant the seed of faith and water it, but Father God, through Holy Spirit brings life. Your situation, issue, problem, infirmity, may seem empty of life, empty of healing; however, what you can do is plant a seed of faith, water it with the Word of God, stand on His promise and have faith and trust in Him. Soon the tiny shoots of life will emerge. You may, however, need to wait on the Lord Jesus, our Master, who in due season causes the springing up, bringing His flourishing resurrection life into your life.

Resurrection testimony

Being a born-again[75] believer from the age of eight, I have heard many testimonies of the miraculous, both local and international; we had visiting speakers at our church regularly. One of those was the 'jellyfish man', Ian McCormack. What struck me about his testimony and has impacted me personally in life is that he prayed the Lord's Prayer in desperation, and that is when his death experience dynamically altered. He had a praying relative, as I remember it. Prayer and intercession are keys to a risen life. This is how Ian's life altering testimony reads, written by Ralph Burden:

75. See Jesus' conversation with Nicodemus in John 3.

Ian McCormack was diving for lobster on the small Island of Mauritius when he was stung by five Box–Jellyfish. Scientists quote this particular type of Jellyfish as being among the most venomous creatures in the world and a sting from a single Box–Jellyfish often proves to be fatal.

'By the time an ambulance arrived my body was totally paralysed and necrosis had begun to set into my bone marrow. On route to the hospital I began to see my life flash before me. I was an atheist – but I knew I was nearly dead and I didn't know if there was life after death or whether there was just nothing,' Ian said.

The ambulance stopped and they placed him in a wheelchair, racing him into the hospital. The nurse took his blood pressure twice but could not find a pulse as his veins had collapsed. The doctors tried to save his life by injecting anti-toxins and dextrose, but to no avail. Within a few minutes Ian slipped into eternity...

'I found myself in a very dark place, not realizing where I was. So, I tried to find a light switch, thinking I was still in the hospital – but as I reached out into the dark, I couldn't touch anything. Reaching to touch my face I found my hand go straight through it. It seemed so bizarre, as I knew I was standing there but couldn't touch any part of my physical body. I began to sense that this wasn't just a physical darkness – there was something else there. I could feel a cold eerie feeling as though something or someone was looking at me. From the darkness I began to hear men's voices screaming at me telling me to "shut up", that "I deserved to be there", that I was 'in Hell".'

Ian couldn't believe it. But as he prayed in desperation, a beam of light shone through the darkness and lifted him upward. He says,

'I felt like a speck of dust being drawn up into a beam of sunlight. I found myself standing in the presence of awesome light and power. I felt pure unadulterated Love flow over me. Love, I thought, how could God love me? I've taken his name in vain, I've slept around, I'm not a good man, but no matter what I said, waves of His unconditional Love continued to flow over me. I found myself weeping uncontrollably in His Presence. I could see a man standing in front of me, but he was not like anyone I'd ever seen before in my life. His garments were shimmering white in colour. I knew I was looking upon God. As I looked toward His face the intensity of the light seemed to increase – you couldn't make out the form of his face as the light was so bright. Moving closer waves of more Love began to flow towards me, and I felt very safe ...I knew I belonged here, that God had created me to live here – I knew I was home.'

But God had other plans for Ian. It wasn't yet time for him to go to heaven.

'I was just about to enter in and explore, when God stepped back in front of me, and asked me this question. "Now that you have seen – do you wish to step in, or do you wish to return?" God then spoke to me and said If I wished to return – I must see things in a new light. I understood that to mean that I must begin to see through his eyes of love, peace, joy, forgiveness, from His Heavenly perspective, not my temporary earthly perspective. Looking back towards the tunnel again I could see a vision of all my family, and

thousands and thousands of other people. I asked God who all these people were, and He told me that if I didn't return then many of these people would not get a chance to hear about Him.'

Ian told God that he did wish to go back for the sake of his mother, and for those who had not yet heard about God's love. So, God sent him back.

'I was lying back on a hospital bed with my right leg elevated, cupped in the hands of the young Indian doctor who had been trying to save my life. He had a scalpel or some sharp instrument in his hand and he was prodding the base of my foot like a dead piece of meat. Something seemed to spook the doctor and he quickly turned his head to see my right eye open, looking at him . . . Terror struck his face, and I got the distinct impression that he felt he has just seen a dead man looking at him . . .'

The medical staff were shocked and amazed to see Ian alive, literally back from the dead! The fact that he awoke at all was an extraordinary miracle.

That same night God completely healed Ian. The next day he discharged himself and walked out of the hospital unaided. Ian went to the beach, where the Creole fishermen who had seen him the day before fled in terror, believing him to be a ghost! Over the next 6 weeks he read the entire Bible.

'I have never been the same and believe that I saw our Lord Jesus Christ in His Glorified form as in Revelation. 1:13 –18.'

Ian's story has been made into a movie entitled 'The Perfect Wave' starring Scott Eastwood, Cheryl Ladd, Rachel Hendrix, Paddy Lister, Jack Halloran, Diana Vickers, Scott Mortensen, Nikolai Mynhardt, Rosy Hodge and Matt Bromley.[76]

76. Ralph Burden, www.reallifestories.org/stories/ianmccormack (accessed 16.1.24). Used with permission.

14

A New Day

Each day fades ...
Rising again at dawn,
The oak unfurls its leaves
Then falling, dying.
Putting out leaves of springtime,
Like the lilies die back ...
Then pushing up
Resurrection shoots of life.

When and where there is great darkness in the earth, so will there be resurrection life springing up; the 'Light of the world' (John 8:12) springs up in our hearts.[77] I love writing and reading poems, and I wrote the poem above after reading the script of one of the early Church fathers:

> Let us consider, beloved, how the Master is continually proving to us that there will be a future resurrection, of which he has made the Lord Jesus Christ the firstling, by raising him from the dead. Let us look, beloved, at the resurrection which is taking place seasonally. Day and night make known the resurrection to us. The night

---

77.   '... pay attention, as with a lamp shining in a dark place, until that Day [the Day of The Lord] would dawn and the Morning Star would rise in your hearts' (2 Peter 1:19).

sleeps, the day arises. Consider the plants that grow. How and in what manner does the sowing take place? The Sower went forth and cast each of the seeds onto the ground; and they fall to the ground, parched and bare, where they decay. Then from their decay the greatness of the master's providence raises them up, and from the one grain more grow and bring forth fruit' (*Letter to the Corinthians* 24:1-6 A.D. 80).[78]

Faith grows, receive a seed gift of faith from the Lord, plant it in your heart and also in the hearts of others, and watch it grow. There is a sense of unfurling in the growth of the faith of the Lord in our hearts. For example, I have heard the teaching concerning 'working the miracle' from a mighty man of God called Robby Dawkins from the US, and also from Mission24 teaching. A person prays once and asks from one to ten, 'how much better is the ailment?' The person being prayed for may answer for example: 'five;' the praying one prays once more, and the ailment goes altogether: a ten out of ten is achieved! Quite often, faith grows, and, more often than not, it grows rapidly in the person praying, and in the person receiving prayer. This is backed up by the biblical account of the miracle of the blind man who could: 'see men that are as trees I see walking.' (Mark 8:24) When being healed by Jesus; the healing grew into a complete miracle step by step.

One morning, the Lord instructed me to read Mark 2, concerning the paralytic who was healed. The creative healing words, which our Messiah Jesus used to heal him were: 'I say to you, you must now rise!' (v. 11). To 'arise', or

---

78. 'What the Early Church Believed: Resurrection of the Body', www.catholic.com/tract/resurrection-of-the-body (accessed 16.1.24).

'awaken' is also used when Jesus says: 'After three days I shall rise' (Matthew 27:63).

The Spirit of the Lord was showing me that our minds need renewing and awakening to the fact that Jesus is risen, and His Spirit is within us continually. We have His authority to cause a rising up in ourselves and others by His Spirit; an awakening, a rising from the dead of the old way of thinking into *the resurrection* knowledge, wisdom, understanding, counsel, awe and might of the Lord (see Isaiah 11). This is one of the reasons Jesus died and rose, so that you and I may: 'Heal the sick, cleanse the lepers, raise the dead' (Matthew 10:8, NKJV).

We can ask for bold faith and patience, which is also required. Keep on moving towards that which the Lord has for you, for it is to bring glory to Him and His name. Jesus, Holy Spirit and Father God, love to see death destroyed on earth, as in heaven; death has already been dealt with on the cross and by the Lord's resurrection and ascension. In 1 Corinthians 6:14, it is written: 'Now God has not only raised the Lord, but will also raise us up through His power' (NASB). This word from our Lord can be applied both to natural and spiritual resurrection. His loving kindnesses are 'new every morning,' and great is His faithfulness to those who love Him (Lamentations 3:23). Arise, O Bride of Messiah, and know that you are seated in 'the heavenlies' (Ephesians 2:6) in His Spirit, to be equipped to even raise the dead.

When we have surrendered our lives to the Lord God in baptism both of water and of Spirit, we have died to the world, and we now live for, and to, an unseen Kingdom; the kingdom of God which Jesus tells us to: 'seek first' (Matthew 6:33) and 'His righteousness'. One of the effects, or 'side effects,' is that we will have a renewal in our bodies, as well as our minds and spirit. This renewal means a supernatural energy at times of natural flagging. Have you experienced this? If you speak in the tongues of heavenly language,[79] continually endeavour to flow in this gifting, especially when you are feeling weary, and watch what happens. Jackie Pullinger, the famed missionary, gives testimony that speaking in tongues enabled people to kick the addictive habit of cocaine use.[80] You will find a springing up of life; this is the arising power of the Lord, who causes us to 'mount up with wings like eagles' (Isaiah 40:31, ESV). Wait upon the Lord and He will renew your strength.[81]

Can you and I receive, give, declare, and activate the resurrection power of the Lord Himself? The disciples were commanded to go and 'Heal the sick, cleanse the lepers, raise the dead' (Matthew 10:8, NKJV) – it stands to reason that we too are enabled to do so. It is the Lord who causes the resurrection from the dead, through His life-giving Spirit, and He asks us to be part of this awesome process. What a huge privilege! The Lord has given us authority to go and raise the dead and, in Jesus, you have authority in every situation. Take a moment to ponder this, receive confidence and boldness in The Spirit when facing any enemy. Jesus has all authority in your situation wherever you are, whatever you face – in your life, in your health, in your finances, so have confidence in His authority. It is written: 'I am with you always,' says the Lord in Matthew 28:20 (NKJV); He is with you in His resurrection power. This power is not only for you but for others: 'Freely you have received, freely give' (Matthew 10:8, NKJV). You are going out in His name, believing other people will know

---

79. 1 Corinthians 12:10.
80. Jackie Pullinger, *Chasing the Dragon* (London: Hodder & Stoughton, 2006).
81. Isaiah 40:31.

that He lives. You have all authority in the name of Jesus, even to raise the dead! In fact, the declaration of Jesus' parting words on earth before He ascended into heavenly realms was:

you will take power when the Holy Spirit comes upon you and you will be My witnesses in Jerusalem in all Judea and Samaria and to the outermost part of the earth.

(Acts 1:8)

Let us be His faithful witnesses. He has died and has risen, so that we can go and declare His good works and do His will, may His Kingdom come, and His will be done ... (see Matthew 6).

Resurrection testimony

Here is a wonderful resurrection testimony to encourage your faith.

Jonathan Conrathe, Mission24 senior leader and evangelist, Milan from Slovakia experienced a resurrection from the dead:[82]

Jonathan related a testimony concerning his dear friend Milan, a Slovakian evangelist who trained with Jonathan on his mission school. The Mission school went on a trip to Uganda. Milan took a team over to a local hospital and was expectant, due to having received a prophecy in his native country that he was

---

82. Jonathan Conrathe, Mission24 Spring teaching. Transcribed by author from Mission24 video, 19.3.22. Edited for the purposes of this book.

going to meet a surgeon in a restaurant who would open the door to the team to go and pray with people. The previous evening this prophecy came to pass when he met the surgeon, who opened up the doors for the team to minister in the hospital. When the team entered the hospital, they saw a wife grieving the loss of her beloved husband who had died a few hours before. He was laid in a side room. 'Could we go and pray with the body?' They asked. The doctor said it was too late, but they could if they wanted to. The team gathered around the body of the husband in the room and rebuked death and commanded life back into the man. After a time of doing this, they felt led to praise God, which they all did for half an hour or so. They focused on God, closing their eyes and lifting up their hands and voices, shouting and praising God with declarations of thanksgiving. Suddenly, one of them heard a sound from the bed, and it was the man who had sat up in bed. The white sheet, which had covered his face and body was discarded, and the husband was reunited with his wife! This is not the end of the testimony because the team went on to pray for many in that hospital in Kampala where two-thirds of the patients were healed miraculously. Their medical records confirmed the healings, and they were sent home! Nearly everyone in that hospital gave their lives to God due to these incredible testimonies and the man being raised from the dead.

During giving this testimony, Jonathan taught us some of the keys to raising the dead from his own experience; though not a formula, they are biblical guidelines. I have paraphrased them here:

- Always respond to faith in yourself, and also of the people around you.
- Obey the Holy Spirit. Follow His leading, and do not give in to the pressure from others who may not be in faith.
- You can receive the commanding authority of the Lord: 'Do not tremble! Do not be dismayed! For the LORD your God is with you wherever you go' (Joshua 1:9).
- You should rebuke the spirit of death ...
- And speak life: command the person's spirit to return to their body in the name of Jesus (remember, though, it is also their will as to whether to return or not).
- Praise God in faith. Thank Him for His resurrection power to enable you to raise the dead.
- Once the person has been raised from the dead, give them food and water.

Remember too, that resurrection from the dead demonstrates the victory and authority of the Lord Jesus Christ, and His power over sin and death, as we read in 1 Corinthians 15.

On reading John 5, 19–29, I found another set of guidelines regarding raising up the dead. Here is the list which Holy Spirit helped me see in this portion of scripture:

- We must do the Father's will as Jesus did.
- Be in love with God the Father, Son, and Holy Spirit, realise His love for us, and the one we are praying for.

- Delegate all judgment to Jesus, do not judge the one we are praying for.
- Honour God, honour each other.
- Listen to God, Holy Spirit and have faith.
- Speak out the words God gives you.
- Obey His voice and actions, seek first God's will.

As we have read, all these testimonies are slightly different, as are the actions and words the saints of God use in each case; there are no hard and fast rules or set formula. It is Father God, through Jesus Christ and His Holy Spirit, who raises the dead. However, God has called us, and has chosen to use *us*, to destroy the works of His, and our enemies, which means being a part of the manifestations of destroying death itself. All glory be to God!

15

The First Resurrection

And those who have done good things
shall go forth into resurrection life.
(John 5:29)

...for it will be repaid to you in the
resurrection of the righteous.
(Luke 14:14)

The First Resurrection is the good news of the kingdom of God on the earth; it is the saints' great hope. The book of Revelation emphasises the return of the Lord Jesus Christ in glory and speaks directly of the First and Second resurrections from the dead. The First Resurrection is spoken of in scripture as the resurrection of the righteous saints, when Jesus our Messiah returns for the second time and thereafter the saints reign with Him for 1,000 years.

> Then I saw thrones, and they sat on them, and judgment was given to them. And I saw the souls of those who had been beheaded because of their testimony of Jesus and because of the word of God, and those who had not worshiped the beast or his image and had not received the mark on their

foreheads and on their hand; and they came to life and reigned with Christ for a thousand years. The rest of the dead did not come to life until the thousand years were completed. This is the first resurrection. Blessed and holy is the one who has a part in the first resurrection; over these the second death has no power, but they will be priests of God and of Christ and will reign with Him for a thousand years.

(Revelation 20:4–6)

Most scholars agree that the righteous dead in Christ rise when Jesus returns the second time to reign for 1,000 years on earth.[83] Some believe that those who have been 'raptured'[84] will walk on earth in their glorified bodies. From the text it seems that most rise to an earthly body first – like Lazarus of Bethany, and then ascend to a glorified body. I have tended to focus in on the life and death of Jesus and the patterning of His death resurrection and ascension in terms of working out the detail of the First Resurrection; due to the fact Jesus Christ is: 'the Author and Finisher' (Hebrews 12:2) of our righteous faith. I would therefore put more emphasis on ascension than 'rapture.' I would add also, that the glory of God, through His Holy Spirit, is affecting our earthly bodies at this moment. As we commune with the Lord and pray and worship, we are filled with His glory; we are transformed from one glory to the next glory,[85] both in the natural and supernatural. Many saints of old experienced this glory of God, even near to their death, such as Stephen, who 'saw the glory of God' (Acts 7:55) and his face had become 'like a face of an

---

83. Isaiah 2:4.
84. 1 Thessalonians 4:16–17.
85. 2 Corinthians 3:18.

angel,' (Acts 6:15) perhaps God's glory shielded him from some of the pain of death by stoning. Our youth can be renewed like the eagle's as we wait on the Lord; He renews our strength,[86] both physically and spiritually.

During giving birth at home to our son, I believe I experienced the resurrection glory power of the Lord surge through my body, saving mine and our son's life. Our baby's shoulders were stuck in the birth canal, and afterwards the midwives testified that they witnessed a miracle. Through the Lord's strength, I was able to rise up to a standing position, even though at the time, I was passing out and it felt as though I was slipping into death. I declared the Lord's Prayer in a whisper continually, after which I knew exactly what to do. Going into action and suddenly waking up, I felt a surge of strength to stand, even though the baby was stuck, which cut off his blood supply and was causing me grievous harm. The witnesses to this knew it was physically impossible for me to have stood up; I was not able to communicate to ask for help. In the natural, my body should not have been able to endure it with the baby stuck half in, half out. God answered my prayers and intervened by His glorious strength, and I was able to raise myself up. I was holding hands with my husband and so he followed my lead to support me to stand up. My son was born healthily, and I have no side effects related to strain to my heart. Praise Him who caused us to rise up!

This glory of God in the flesh may also be that which Enoch and Elijah experienced.[87] In both cases maybe there was a seeking the Lord with all their heart, soul and body; a drawing intentionality to be with the Lord where He is:

---

86. Isaiha 40:31.
87. Genesis 5:24; 2 Kings 2:11.

high and lifted up, exalted, ascended. The word 'ascended' simply means to be taken up to a higher place (which is similar to the meaning of 'rapture'). May we all have a zeal like Enoch and Elijah for seeking the Lord in the fullness of our being. These men were so enraptured by the Lord that they appear to have ascended to heaven in the flesh.

Let us look at Jesus' resurrection alongside the First Resurrection. Jesus rose from his earthly body into a fresh new body. After Jesus went down into Sheol, or Hades, He returned to the earth, appearing to His disciples for forty days. He ate and drank with the disciples in His invigorated resurrected body.[88] Jesus had flesh and bone, though He was able to walk through walls and asked Mary not to touch Him as He had 'not yet ascended' to His Father (John 20:17). His fleshly 'invigorated' body could overcome the laws of physics on the earth. Thomas was able to touch His scars,[89] and many witnessed His presence.

He then ascended to the right hand of the Father God. It is perhaps in the process of ascension that His 'body' was glorified? Similarly, believers, whether in the grave, or alive on earth at the time, will have any bodily remains transformed into their new glorified body when they ascend into heaven. In my view, the transformed fleshly body of the First Resurrection will primarily a human rather than an ascended glorified body; however, a theoretical idea I have had is that the glory of the Lord will cause the resurrected body to be similar to that of Adam and Eve at the beginning, before the Fall; a healed and more 'spiritual' body. I am not wholly sure about this and as Paul writes

---

88. '…for a spirit does not have flesh and bones as you see that I have' (Luke 24:39, NASB).
89. John 20:27.

in 1 Corinthians 15:35, we cannot concern ourselves with details of how the dead will be raised. In the end, it is a mystery of which Father God knows all the answers. We can trust in Father God. Like a child, it is fine to have our ideas, theories and to wonder; however, we must not make a point of arguing over such things. The difference between our body and Jesus' body is that He was begotten from heaven, and we are made 'from dust of the earth' (1 Corinthians 15:47).

While writing this chapter, the apostle Paul's words from Philippians were highlighted to me by the Holy Spirit:

> For our citizenship is in the heavens, out from which then we have been waiting eagerly a Savior for ourselves, Lord Y'shua Messiah, who will transform our lowly body to the same form as His glorious body through the power that enables Him to subject everything to Himself... stand firm in the Lord...
>
> *(Philippians 3:20 – 4:1)*

> Stand firm in the knowledge that as your faith in Yeshua, Jesus your Christ, your Messiah grows; you will be transformed in Spirit, in mind, and in glorious body.
>
> *(Romans 12:1-2, my paraphrase)*

Two witnesses

There is a prophetic resurrection testimony in the book of Revelation which precedes the 'First Resurrection'. It is the resurrection of the two witnessing saints detailed in Revelation 11, who some say represent Israel and the Gentile nations.

The identity of the two witnesses is mysterious, with some clues. There are two schools of thought, many believe Elijah, and the spirit of Elijah, to be ushering in the second coming of the Lord. And they believe Moses is the second witness, whilst others believe that Enoch is the second man who appears.[90] Enoch ascended to heaven 'in the flesh,' and therefore has not yet died in his flesh. He is thought to be coming back as the second witness to die a martyr's death; then to be raised up and ascended.

These two witnesses die in the streets as they give testimony of Jesus. It is written in John's gospel that 'Even in your Law [Torah teaching] it has been written that the testimony of two people is true' (John 8:17, NASB). The two witnesses will be persecuted unto death by their enemies on earth because they give testimony of God, and they will torment the unbelieving earth dwellers with plagues, signs and wonders. The breath of life from God thereafter enters these holy witnesses and they stand on their feet, being raised from the dead; a 'great fear' will fall 'upon those who saw them' (Revelation 11:11).

> And they heard a great voice from heaven saying unto them, Come up hither. And they ascended up to heaven in a cloud; and their enemies beheld them.
>
> *(Revelation 11:12, KJV)*

Afterwards, in Revelation 13, the two beasts appear; one an evil prophet who aids the anti-God/Christ, and the

---

90. 'Enoch'. 'From the Bible, we know that Enoch was seventh from Adam, his great-grandson [x 4] (and Noah's great-grandfather) who lived a holy and faithful life to the Lord. He also became the father of Methuselah, the longest-living man. Throughout his three-plus centuries on earth [365 years], he had numerous other offspring. Enoch is also only one of two people taken straight to heaven, escaping death altogether.' See Hebrews 11:5; www.christianity.com/wiki/bible/who-was-enoch-in-the-bible.html (accessed 17.1.24).

other, the anti-Christ himself. Looking at the ripple of patterning from the Old Testament; there is a doubling up. Two holy witnesses and two evil proponents. Biblically, the number two can mean union and also division; a man and a woman become one from two in the union of marriage, and two or more witnesses are needed for a court of law. The resurrection miracle of the two witnesses reminds me of a coming union of all things whether 'Jewish or Greeks or slaves or free' (1 Corinthians 12:13): in 'One New Man' (Ephesians 2:15). The two witnesses are depicted in Zechariah 4:14 (Revelation 11:4) as two olive trees linked by a Menorah. Menorah are also depicted at the beginning of the book of Revelation as the seven churches (the one Bride of Christ).

Fire is called down from heaven by the witnesses, which reminds us of Elijah calling down the fire on the altar in the famous show of God's glory to the prophets of Baal in 1 Kings 18; the skies are closed, harkening back to 1 Kings 17:1, where God stopped up the heavens through Elijah and water is turned to blood; reminiscent of the Exodus plagues of Egypt. All these actions, miracles and wonders are in order to turn the unbelieving peoples of earth to God; to know that He is God and to cause them to repent of all evil; to turn back to Him and His righteousness, before the second coming of Jesus the Messiah. These signs and wonders are a judgement of God, the consequence of the people's unbelief in the one true God and His witnesses: His messengers. One of the first mentions in all of Scripture of 'signs' is as follows:

if they will not believe even these two signs nor pay attention to what you say, then you shall take some water from the Nile and pour it on the dry ground; and

129

the water which you take from the Nile will turn into blood on the dry ground.

(Exodus 4:9, NASB)

The Lord God mentions a number of times in Exodus: 'Then the Egyptians shall know that I am the LORD' (Exodus 7:5, NASB). This is in context of showing them His great judgements by way of signs and wonders in the ten plagues. This is so that unbelievers, including the Egyptians, would become believers and worshippers of *the* one true God.

Millenium

Therefore, with regards the First Resurrection, all those who have overcome and are a part of the Bride of Christ from the First Resurrection, will join the 1,000 years reign of Jesus Christ. Whether this be on earth or in heaven is a matter of scriptural interpretation. 1 Thessalonians 4:16 and 17 have been used to interpret a heavenly 1,000-year reign:

> … and the dead in Christ shall rise first. Then we who are alive, who remain, will be caught up together with them in the clouds to meet the Lord in the air, and so we will always be with the Lord.
>
> *(NASB)*

Other scholars believe that Revelation 20:4 is speaking about the rule and reign of Messiah on earth. This seems to make more sense in terms of the resurrection teaching of the Bible as a whole, as well as patterning. For instance,

Jesus resurrected from the dead and remained forty days, before ascending on high. Isaiah also writes of a time in the future when 'the knowledge and glory of God would cover the earth,' in Isaiah 11:6, where 'a little child will lead' ... 'the calf and the young lion ... together' (NKJV).

I personally believe that the 1,000-year reign of Messiah will be a time of teaching and celebrating the God-given feasts in the Word of God, whether on earth or in heaven is debatable. Jesus, the Son of God, will lead us and teach us about how to live the holy life that the Father God had designed for all humanity. Israel, having been a prototype nation, whom God asked to follow His way of living, had failed in the past (much like many Christians). Jesus' first coming gave a new promise of salvation, of spiritual freedom to eternal life and Messiah Jesus is returning a second time, as the King and Judge of all and a teacher to all nations who have surrendered their lives to Him, choosing His way of life.[91]

In the Millenium rest, we, the Bride of Messiah, will be celebrating our betrothal during the wedding feast, being taught the righteous way to live in holiness and purity. Jesus Himself will be our role model and ever-present Rabbi, which means Teacher. The tabernacle of David will be wholly restored. Read Isaiah 2:2-4 where it is written that in the last days, the nations will flock to the 'mountain of the LORD' and 'He will teach us His Ways and we will walk in His paths; for the Torah (Teaching) will go out from Zion'.

The 1,000-year reign of Jesus Messiah's kingdom is also a Jubilee rest from the life of trial, toil and persecution of the previous earthly sixth millennia. It will be the seventh millennia of Sabbatical Jubilee rest.

---

91. Deuteronomy 30:19.

During the 1,000-year reign of Messiah, there seems to be free will, and consequently those who choose to disobey God. There is a description in the Bible of a place for those judged and found unworthy at the wedding feast of the Lamb. Matthew 22 outlines Jesus' parable of the marriage feast which shows people being removed:

Friend, how did you enter here not having a wedding garment? . . . you must cast him into the furthest darkness: in that place there will be weeping and gnashing of the teeth.

(Matthew 22:12–13)

The place of further or 'outer darkness' seems to be a place where people are sent *before* they experience the Great White Throne judgement of God found in Revelation 20. Perhaps this is a place of repentance, and that they have one final opportunity to turn their lives around for good?

After the 1,000-year reign of Jesus, Revelation 20 tells us the enemy of the Lord, and of His saints will be let loose one final time and the righteous will ascend to be with the Lord.[92] It is then that our bodies will be transformed to a fully glorious heavenly state:

Lord Y'shua Messiah ... will transform our lowly body to the same form as His glorious body through the power that enables Him to subject everything to Himself.

(Philippians 3:20–21)

---

92. Author views on rapture, and acknowledgment that others may believe differently.

According to the book of Revelation timeline of events, the enemy, Satan, is let loose on the earth for a short time before the Great White Throne judgement. Thereafter comes the wrapping up of heaven and earth, to make way for the new heavenly city, which comes down from heaven to a new earth.

One wonderful day, all will be revealed; the Lord Himself will show us which scholars had the correct emphasis and balance concerning resurrection, ascension and rapture; and where we are on the timeline of history presently with regards the end of days. The revelation of Jesus our Messiah will be fully explained; nothing added, and nothing taken away. Until that day, it is a wise scribe who does not add nor take away from the revelation of Jesus Messiah.

Resurrection testimony

Rod Lewis is a pastor and evangelist who has this resurrection testimony to share with us:[93]

> One February morning in 1985, it had snowed heavily so I went out to clear the path. Suddenly, I felt a sharp pain like a knife in my back. I shouted for Pauline [Rod's wife] to come and help me; she and one of my daughters rushed to get me into the house. Pauline ran to the neighbours for help. By the time she returned I was sitting on a chair – and then I died in front of them both.
>
> Meanwhile I had the sensation of travelling at high speed through a tunnel. My natural senses were

---

93. Rod Lewis, 11.5.23 (email testimony 2022). His testimony can be viewed at https://drrichardkent.org/?s=rod+lewis (accessed 17.1.24). Edited for the purposes of this book.

heightened: the colours were more vivid, my hearing acute. I had no fear, I knew I was travelling to heaven. I saw before me the brilliant, radiant glory of heaven. Suddenly, I heard the name 'Jesus!' echoing through the tunnel, three times. Back I came through the tunnel at top speed; returning to my body. I became aware of Pauline praying one word: 'Jesus!' She told me [later] that was all she could say! I opened my eyes and was so grateful for the extraordinary power of the name of Jesus that brought me back from the dead.

I spent several days in hospital where they diagnosed furring of arteries to the brain. However, with further X-rays there was no sign of the damage, and my blood flow was normal. I had been healed! God has given me a specific ministry in seeing other people raised back to life.

For example, later that year, at church on a Sunday evening in October, I was preaching a message from Psalm 133: 'How good it is when God's people gather together in unity, for it commands a blessing.' I spoke about it being like anointing oil being poured out. Suddenly, a congregant came rushing to the front and said: 'Pastor, come quick, someone has collapsed!' A man was lying on the floor, completely lifeless. The congregant said to me: 'Pastor, hold out your hands.' When I did so, she poured a bottle of oil over my hands and told me to slap it on the man's head! As I did that, an anointing came from God upon me. I declared: 'Spirit of death, I rebuke you! In the name of Jesus, [life], come back into your body!' Instantly, his colour returned to his face, he opened his eyes. 'Is that you?' I asked of the congregant. 'Yes,' he replied. The paramedics were amazed to find the man alive and fine. As God promises, when we come together in unity there is a special blessing! What a mighty God we serve.

Here is another great testimony from a congregant from Rod's Church:

I was serving as a lay minister in August 2008 at a wedding between two of our church members. I saw Rod Lewis come into church. 'Hello Rod, great to see you here. Do you know the bride or groom?' Rod replied: 'No, I am not really sure why I am here; last night as I was preparing a sermon on Romans 8, focusing on the resurrection power of the Lord, the Lord told me to come here this morning.' When the time came for the wedding ceremony, the bride's father, who was giving away his daughter, suddenly collapsed with a heart attack. His daughter, who is a nurse, was giving him CPR but her father was unresponsive. The next thing I knew, Rod was standing over the man and commanding life to return. The man then opened his eyes and began to sit up! What a turn around. When the paramedics came, they could find nothing wrong, and the dad left the hospital with a full bill of health. I do fully believe this was a divine move of the Lord because of what I witnessed, but perhaps more so because of my conversation with Rod before any events unfolded.[94]

Thank You, Lord, for raising the dead through the actions and prayers of Your people.

---

94. Edited for the purposes of this book.

16

The Second Resurrection

———◆———

Be in awe of the Lord.
For the dead shall arise.
To glory or everlasting shame:
Eternal flame,
Forever blamed.
Humble yourself
Under the Mighty hand of God
Before you depart.

This second resurrection will appear at the very end of the age. Those to be raised from the dead are those who have gone down into Sheol/Hades throughout the ages.[95]

> ... I saw the dead, the great and the small, standing before the throne, and scrolls were opened, and another scroll was opened, which is of life ... and the dead were judged according to their deeds ... Then the sea gave up the dead that were in it, and Death and Hades gave up the dead, those in them, and each was judged according to his works. Then Death and Hades were thrown violently into the lake of fire. This is

---

95. www.blueletterbible.org/lexicon/g1067/amp/mgnt/0-1/ Strongs G1067 (accessed 25.1.24)

the second death, the lake of fire. And if someone was not found written in the Book of Life, he was cast into the lake of fire.

(Revelation 20:12–15)

People will be raised to go to God's Great White Throne judgement spoken of in Revelation 20. John writes in verse 5 that: 'The rest of the dead did not come to life until the thousand years were completed' (NASB). The 'rest of the dead' appear to be those who are the unrighteous or 'unsaved' by Messiah Jesus. After these judgements, there shall be no more death or sorrow for those who are the righteous of God.[96]

During the second resurrection, the rest of humankind is raised up; every bone and sinew and blood that has been spilt over the ages will be transformed and thereafter all souls judged. 'For the life of the flesh is in the blood' (Leviticus 17:11, KJV). All people must account for their deeds and be judged by our holy Father God.

Many scholars[97] agree that the second resurrection is, in emphasis, for those who are immoral, wicked and who do not believe in God; and they will be resurrected into incorruptible bodies, in order to experience 'the lake of fire' eternally, which is written of in Revelation 21. They will be sent to eternal suffering. In summary, there are the righteous who are raised into glory in the First Resurrection and the unrighteous who are cast into perpetual fire at the Second Resurrection.[98]

96. Revelation 21:4.
97. https://biblical-christianity.com/the-first-and-second-resurrection (accessed 25.1.24)
98. See https://bible.knowing-jesus.com/topics/Second-Resurrection (accessed 17.1.24).

This causes an awe of the Lord within us; the Lord Almighty has the ability to judge each one of us and to save us *or* to release us into eternal suffering. The saved can rejoice that our names are written in the Lamb's Book of Life, but we should not be prideful of the power the Lord has bestowed upon and within us. We are humbled by *His* righteous judgement as King of all kings. The Second Resurrection is a motivation to show others around us, the saving grace of our Lord Jesus Christ and to encourage our neighbours to know Jesus as Messiah, and to become part of His First Resurrection.

After the White Throne Judgement, a new heaven and a new earth will be created, as well as a new city called the 'New Jerusalem' or 'Zion'. This city, complete with all the righteous people of God, will descend down out of the heavenly realms, full of the ascended saints. The New Jerusalem descends as the fully betrothed Bride of Messiah.[99] The people in and out of this new city are those of the resurrection from the dead.

This time, instead of Adam and Eve populating the earth gradually as with the 'old earth,' people from every tribe and nation, who have been transformed into their heavenly glorified bodies and have one mind, soul and spirit, populate the new earth. These are the fully betrothed and are continually abiding with Father, Son and Spirit. All these people will descend together as the New Jerusalem into the newly created earth. These are the ones whose names have been written in the Lamb's Book of Life.[100] Let us be in awe of the Lord who decides our ultimate, eternal

---

99. 'And I saw the holy city, new Jerusalem, coming down out of heaven from God, prepared as a bride adorned for her husband' (Revelation 21:2, NASB).
100. Revelation 20 11:15; see also, 'nothing unclean, and no one who practices abomination and lying, shall ever come into it, but only those whose names are written in the Lamb's book of life.' (Revelation 21:27, NASB).

destination; let each one of us to desire to be righteous, just and true, like Jesus.

The good news is that you and I now still have the chance, and the choice to believe in the Lord Jesus and all that He has achieved, and to be saved, repent, be baptised and live in His resurrection life until we die to this earth, to live with Him in heavenly realms; to 'live and move and have our being' (Acts 17:28) in Him. We are commissioned by Jesus to go and spread the good news of His saving grace and powerful love.

Prayer

Lord, I surrender my whole self to You: body, mind and spirit.
Thank You for forgiving me for all disobedience, lies, and everything which goes against Your commands.
Please forgive me for everything I have done wrong.
I turn away from those things and with Your help, do not want to do them again.
I want to walk through life led by Your Spirit.
I want to do the right thing, to seek after *Your* righteousness, peace and joy.
Holy Spirit, come into my heart and cleanse me.
Turn my life around. Make me new.
Write and keep my name in Your book of life, I pray.
Thank You for Your promise of being with me until the end.
In Jesus' name I pray.
Amen.

I believe the acts of lovingkindness we do contribute to making the beautiful garments we will wear during the wedding feast. We are all invited, through Jesus' incredible invitation, to be with the Bridegroom of all bridegrooms; through our relationship with Him individually and collectively, to be betrothed to Him and celebrate our eternal home together, forever with Him.

I like to find patterns in the Scriptures. Ascending and descending patterns can be found when Jesus, Messiah ascends and descends (I have excluded the Transfiguration, where Jesus met Elijah and Moses).[101] Below is how I currently view the patterning:

1. Jesus came down as a baby from heaven to earth.

2. He died, went down to Sheol/Hades (Ghenna or Hellfire happens at the final judgement).

3. Messiah Jesus arose and appeared for forty days to His disciples. He then ascended from earth to heaven.

4. He is coming again from heaven to earth for a second time.

5. His Bride of believers rise in the First Resurrection to live on earth, (or in heaven[102]) during the restful Millennium reign of Messiah with any believers who survived the tribulation.

6. The enemy will be let loose for a short time after the 1,000 year reign. The Second Resurrection will occur, raising those who are unrighteous.

7. The Great White Throne judgement happens in heaven, and everyone is caught up into heaven: righteous and unrighteous to be judged. The old

---

101. See Matthew 17.
102   Many Christians believe that the Millenium reign happens in heaven.

earth is rolled up and death dealt with, once and for all.

8. Our Bridegroom Jesus then descends with His Bride collectively in triumph once more to a new earth, from a new heavenly realm. It is written, at this point that 'sorrow and sighing will flee away' (Isaiah 51:11, NASB) and there be 'no more death' (Revelation 21:4, KJV).

There are two more possible types of ascending and descending; these and others could be said to be 'messianic' or 'Angel of the LORD' or 'Christophany' experiences mentioned in Scripture:

1. The Lord God walked with Adam and Eve in the Garden.

2. The Messiah descended to talk with Abraham.

3. The Messiah came down to talk with Moses at the burning bush.

4. The Angel of the Lord spoke with Joshua regards Jericho.

5. The Messiah's back was shown to Moses on the mountain.

6. The Angel of the Lord struggled with Jacob.

7. Yeshua appeared to Paul on the road to Damascus.

8. Yeshua gave His revelation to John on Patmos.

And there are probably other wonderful patterns to discover in the Scriptures.

Resurrection testimony

The following is the testimony of the near-death experience of Christine Eastell, who lives in the UK, and has worked closely with Dr Richard Kent, author of *The Final Frontier*.[103]

Christine considered herself a Christian at the time of her experience. However, interestingly, she had not surrendered herself fully to Jesus Christ. She was focusing her life on her career more than seeking after God and a life of faith in Him.

... On the 11th December 1989, my life was changed completely. I was suffering from a very bad dose of influenza. Instead of being sensible, and going to bed, I decided to go into work. Everyone I went to see told me I was crazy, and should not be working at all. But I said I was OK. The real reason was that I had just had another career jump. In this new position I was not entitled to any sick pay. Of course the life style I had become used to necessitated high expenditure each month, so that even one day's pay was too much to give up.

By the afternoon I was feeling extremely ill. I had been driving for most of the day, which was wet, windy and foggy. Every bad driving condition you could think of. Even to contemplate driving myself home was madness, but I still tried. Then, during one moment's lack of concentration, I wandered slightly over the central white line, and hit the only car on the road coming in the opposition direction. Such was the impact that it took a long time to get me out of the car.

103. Richard Kent, *The Final Frontier* (Grand Rapids, MI: Zondervan/Marshall Pickering, 1997).

. . . God's hand was certainly upon me, and the situation, because the driver of the car I hit should have had exactly the same injuries as myself. He escaped with just a cut lip and some whiplash. We had exactly the same model car and had been travelling at the same speed. In a head on crash of this nature, both drivers would normally receive similar injuries. He however, got out of his car, and was able to walk without any problems. How good God is! Had the other driver been injured in the same way as I had been, his life could have been in ruins, and I would have been responsible.

I did not learn until sometime later how seriously injured I had been. At first I felt nothing in the way of pain. Yet it would be easier to list what I had not broken and cut! I was in a terrible mess, and was lacerated all over my body. Not only was my car that was a total write-off, but I was as well. The time in Casualty was vague and unreal, as if it was happening to someone else. Over the next few days my condition deteriorated. The broken bones were not the major problem. My internal injuries were causing the serious concern. On two occasions I had a cardiac arrest, and I had to be resuscitated. It was all systems go, with everybody rushing to my aid. I had gone into septicaemic shock due to the internal damage.

I was taken to the Intensive Care Unit and wired up to machines. The prognosis was such that I had to have someone beside me all the time. My three grown up daughters were there. My parents also came. They were given a room in the hospital. The staff told them to sit and talk to me, but they did not know if I could hear anything. They were resigned to the fact that I was going to die, perhaps even within a few hours. I remained in that state for seven days, and that in many ways is where my testimony begins.

Whilst I was in this limbo state, with the machines in effect keeping my body alive, my spirit left my body. It was very clear, and I know it was not hallucinations caused by the drugs I was on.

When my spirit began to leave my body I began to go down into a very deep pit ... There was no beginning or end, and no sides. I just knew I was in a pit. I kept closing my eyes, and hoping that when I opened them it would all be a bad dream, but nothing changed. It is impossible to find words to describe the fear I felt. I was desperate to get out. When I saw what I thought was a small opening I began to claw desperately. But the more I tried to get to this opening, the more distant it became. It was an impossible situation.

All around there were people, just ordinary people. They were in deep pain and despair, and they seemed to be tormented by an enormous sense of guilt ... It is so difficult to describe the depth of despair that was present in that place. If you could put all the pain, hurt and despair in the world together, then that was what I sensed in that place.

... In the darkness I became aware of an even more evil presence than I had already felt ... In my terror I screamed out, 'I am a Christian, and I belong to Jesus, I should not be here' ... What could I do? There I was in Hell,[104] with Satan, and in total despair. I had thought I was a Christian, but I had not committed my life to Jesus.

---

104. This may be Sheol/Hades not 'Hell.' Please see below: 'Near Death, Now Restored' and notes 107 and 118.

At that point I thought, 'Lord, please rescue me'. I prayed for forgiveness, and I remember falling on my knees pleading with Him to forgive me ... Then I stayed there, because I could not do anything else. But, praise God, Satan is a defeated enemy.

Jesus heard my prayer, and He lifted me up ... into His presence. I looked up, and there stood Jesus in all His glory ... This was so different to the place I had come from, and now I was in the presence of Jesus. I could feel His love and His peace ...

As I looked down I saw myself once again in a hospital bed, hooked up to machines, with all my family sitting around. I thought to myself, 'Do I really want to go back?' Whilst I wanted to stay with Jesus, I also loved my family and knew I must return. As I began to come down, as it were, and return to my body, I knew without any shadow of doubt that I was going to get well ...

I was taken off the critical list. Exactly one month later I was discharged from hospital. Once I was taken out of Intensive Care I was put into a side ward. Every day medical staff would come to visit me. They would talk and smile at me. I was not sure what was going on, because I was still very ill. At that stage, I did not realise the impact I had made on all these people. My knees were very badly damaged and were encased in plaster. Every now and then I would be taken down to the Orthopaedic Ward to get my plaster changed. They would say, 'Oh, you're Christine! We have heard about you'. I even got a mention in one of the medical journals.

... After I left hospital I went to stay with my parents, as I needed time to regain my strength. Within three months I was strong enough to return home. I was totally healed. Every bone had knitted well.

When the accident had taken place, the impact was such that it very badly crushed my knees. I thought I would be left with a permanent limp and that I would never be able to kneel again, or climb stairs. Now I have no limp, and I can kneel. In fact I manage to do everything, including my garden! I now work in a Christian bookshop that has 13 stairs, and I go up and down numerous times a day without any problems whatsoever.'[105]

---

105. Christine Eastell, https://drrichardkent.org/books/the-final-frontier-ebook/the-story-of-christine-eastell-uk/ (accessed 30.1.24).

17

Near Death, Now Restored

For if we have been planted together
in the likeness of His death,
we shall be also in the likeness
of His resurrection...

(Romans 6:5, KJV)

There are millions testimonies and reports of 'near-death experiences' (NDE), where a man or woman dies, and their consciousness, or spirit, separates and moves into the dimensions of heaven or Sheol/Hades[106] – and thereafter they return back into their bodies, with a transformed perspective to life on earth.

In recent times, much has been written of individual subjective happenings. There is also an older documentary film found online, called *The Lazarus Phenomenon,* which is all about near-death experiences. In the film, experts are shown to have researched that 12-15 million Americans alone have been recorded and documented to have experienced an NDE. Dr Melvin Morse worked at Seattle Children's Hospital, said that there have been three major

---

106. Some might term this experience 'hell' (Ghenna in Hebrew) although it is debatable whether it is 'hell' or the underworld, known as Sheol (Hebrew) or Hades (Greek). Perhaps there are various places in 'hell' as there are in heaven (throne room, court, glass sea)?

scientific studies into NDEs in the last decades. All of the results of these studies point to the reality of the dying experience of millions of people. Dr Tony Lawrence of Coventry University concurs with Dr Morse in the film, that the 'consistency of similarity of the millions of NDE accounts make probability these are real experiences and not drug induced hallucinations; nor a "brain reaction", which is an old theory easily debunked'.[107] Dr Kent, whom I have spoken with online, and who has given permission to include some testimonies in this book, has studied more than 300 accounts of dying experiences which include near-death experiences of visits to heaven and hell.

For me, one of the main questions concerning these happenings: are these experiences biblical? I am of the opinion that we can find evidence of such an experience in the Apostle Paul's life; for example, in Acts 14 and 2 Corinthians 12.

Paul, a Roman Jew, experienced many trials and persecutions after a dramatic conversion, where he saw a blinding light in which he heard the audible voice of the Lord Jesus. During one major persecution, he was stoned by Jewish people from Antioch and Iconium. They dragged him out of the city thinking that he was dead. The One New Man version of the Bible mentions that it could have been that Paul died in Acts 14:19. The footnote of verse 20: 'Could it be that Paul had died, and when the disciples circled him, praying, that he was restored to life? It certainly seems impossible that someone taken for dead could simply get up and walk away...' (ONM footnote 1, Acts 14:20). There is also the fact that in those days, stoning was used as a

---

107. www.youtube.com/watch?v=cmrzgRrhXYM&t=606s (accessed 17.1.24).

method of biblical judgement and therefore the stoning he experienced would have been unto death. The One New Man version of the Bible directly links the timeline of fourteen years before, in Acts 14 with 2 Corinthians 12:2, where Paul details 'visions and revelations' (2 Corinthians 12:1, ESV) and his famous words: 'whether in the body or out of the body I do not know, God knows', and that he was 'caught up to the third heaven' (v. 2, ESV). Perhaps Paul was describing what the modern world calls: a type of 'NDE?'

If such incredible visions, revelations and 'out of body' happenings took place with apostle Paul, why not other believers in our Lord Jesus Christ?

Resurrection testimony

The following is a testimony from Dr Richard Kent's website written by Gerald Dunphy of Ireland who had a near-death experience.

This was a headache of mammoth proportions! On the 20th May 1982, I was at home in bed…My wife had gone to town…As the morning wore on, the headache grew even worse, until suddenly I felt something snap in my head. I didn't know what it was, but I knew it was serious.

Knowing I needed help, I called out to God. There were a number of things not right in my life, so I promised, 'If I get through this problem, I'll straighten them out.' I then crawled back to my bedroom, got to the window, and called out to my neighbours, who were outside at the time, for help.

An ambulance took me to hospital. I was examined, and had a lumbar puncture. The diagnosis was a brain haemorrhage. In the end it turned out to be a burst artery. I was transferred to the regional hospital, where the specialist arranged for a CAT scan. I had an angiogram the next morning, and woke up nine hours later in the recovery room after surgery. Then I lapsed into a coma. The prognosis was poor.

I was put onto a life support machine. As the clock ticked on I slipped into a deeper and deeper coma. Evidently I was in that coma for days with no change, except that the specialist told my wife I did not have fully fixed or dilated pupils. My wife did not understand the medical terms so asked a cousin of hers, who was a nursing sister. She said that basically I was on the brink of death. The cousin asked my wife if she had ever heard of the healing power of God. She told her about a couple of miracles she had seen, and gave her a telephone number.

That night my wife rang the number and spoke to a man, who was the [previous] President of the Full Gospel Business Men's Fellowship International.[108] When she told him the problem there was a moment's silence. Then he said, 'Mrs. Dunphy, your husband will recover.' Somehow my wife knew, deep down, that his words were true.

Al then asked for three days of prayer and fasting. My wife's cousin contacted as many people as she could, requesting their prayer support. It was put out on the local radio's Christian programme, and prayer groups around the country were contacted. That

108. www.fgbmfi.org/ (accessed 25.1.24).

Sunday evening all of my family gathered to pray for me. The family members were all Catholics, but this kind of meeting was new to them. It was a last resort! What my wife did not know at that time was that all my family had actually gathered to say their goodbye to me. My brother had even come over from England.

The night after the prayer meeting, my wife and her cousin came to visit. They noticed a slight change in my condition. Evidently when they spoke to me, my eyelids fluttered. The cousin went out and spoke with the people monitoring my condition, and asked if there had been any change. They replied that there had not been. Two hours after they left the hospital contacted them. I was conscious. I knew where I was, what had happened to me and even my name!

That evening however, I developed bacterial pneumonia. I had a tracheotomy in an effort to clear my lungs. Coming out of surgery I slipped back into a coma.

The man [whom my wife had spoken to before], had not given up. He came into the hospital, toting a big Bible. He and my wife came into the Intensive Care Unit, where he prayed for me. He put his hands on me and began praying. He prayed quietly for a few minutes, and then began to pray for healing. As he did, my wife could feel heat coming from within my chest, and my eyelids began to flicker just as they had done on the previous Sunday. Then I heard the Full Gospel man say, 'You know who's here, don't you?' I nodded my head, and he gave a prayer of thanksgiving. I put my hands together and endeavoured to mouth the words he prayed.

Of course I was aware of very little of what went on during that time, as far as the hospital and surroundings were concerned. What I do know is that during the second coma I had a sensation of my spirit leaving my body. I felt drawn to a light at the end of a long tunnel. To my left I saw a white horse in full gallop. Then I came to a tunnel to the right. I stopped in front of it and heard a voice. It asked me three questions about my love for my wife and children, after which it went on to say that love was the key to the kingdom. It also said I would have to come back to Earth. I then returned to my body and regained consciousness.

The following day I was awake and alert. Three days later when the chest specialist returned, he was delighted to see me up from my bed and walking about. Two weeks later I was released from hospital.

Out of gratitude, my wife started attending prayer meetings regularly. They continued to pray for me. Nine months later I asked my wife to get a babysitter so that I could come with her to the prayer meeting that night.

About a year later, we went to a Full Gospel Business Men's Fellowship Convention. On the Saturday evening I went to the front and asked one of the men to pray for me. I committed my life to Jesus Christ that night.

As he continued to pray for me, I reached into my pocket, took out my cigarettes, threw them on the floor, and stamped on them. I had tried unsuccessfully to stop smoking before. Since that time I have not touched a cigarette. The urge to smoke went completely.

Before this experience, my whole life was in a mess. If God had not stepped in, my wife and I would surely have separated. In the period after my miraculous healing and my commitment to Jesus, God began dealing with my problems one by one. From that time I have experienced God's help and guidance in all areas of my life, particularly in the fulfilling of a dream I had of opening a Christian book shop in my spare time. God has wonderfully enabled that to happen, and I am able to give Bibles away free to new people in our prayer group. God has changed our lives in so many ways. He is truly a wonderful and loving Father.[109]

---

109. https://drrichardkent.org/books/the-final-frontier-ebook/the-story-of-gerard-dunphy-ireland/ (accessed 21.1.24). Edited for the purposes of this book.

18

Resurrection Prayers

Glory Be
To Him
Who Died and Rose
For Me
Who Has
The Victory
Over Death

Prayer is a key to the resurrected life. Prayer is the continual communing with the Lord daily. We are called individually and corporately to be a House of Prayer to the nations.[110] In the search for specific resurrection prayers, I looked to Jesus and the prayers He would have prayed while on earth.

'Yeshua' is the Hebrew name for Jesus which means 'salvation'. In his day, Yeshua would have prayed at least three times daily. He would have prayed the 'Amidah' or the 'Shemonaih Esrei', which is one of the most important prayers for Jewish people; it is said that this is where our Lord's Prayer comes from. The second portion of these original eighteen sections of prayer was called: 'God's Might' and much of it refers to the resurrection of the

---

110. Isaiah 56:7.

dead. Here are some beautiful portions which magnify
our Messiah:

> You are mighty forever, my Master
> You resurrect the dead —
> You are mighty to save.
> You sustain the living with lovingkindness,
> resurrecting the dead with great compassion;
> Supporter of the fallen,
> and Healer of the sick;
> Releaser of the imprisoned
> and Fulfiller of His Faithfulness
> to those asleep in the dust…
> …And You are faithful.
> to restore life to the dead.
> Blessed are you Adonai,
> Resurrector of the dead…[111]
> Amen.

These original Jewish prayers are very powerful declarations,
which are full of encouraging faith and hope. We can also
find declarations of resurrection power in the Psalms, which
seem to come from the heart of Messiah Jesus, as if He
is praying to God the Father about His own resurrection.
We too can pray and declare concerning the eternal life
Jesus, our Messiah has purchased for us with great cost.
David writes:

> For You will not commit My life to the grave, neither will
> You permit Your Pious One to see corruption.
>
> *(Psalm 16:10)*

---

111. *Siddur Tehillot Ha Mashiach (Praises of the Messiah)*, Erev Shabbat Morning
      Service, pp. 61–62, Torahresource 2008, www.torahresource.com (accessed
      5.2.24).

Peter quotes this verse in Acts 2 twice[112] concerning the resurrection of the Lord Yeshua; we have the hope of resurrection to eternal life because of that which our Lord has achieved for us.

Some of our early Church fathers and saints prayed to the Lord about His resurrection. Here are some of their prayers. Let us be inspired by these prayers and continue to meditate and pray as we read. This is the prayer of St Gregory the Great:

Dear Lord Jesus Christ,
You paid the debt of Adam for us to the Eternal Father
by Your Blood poured forth in loving-kindness.
You cleared away the darkness of sin by Your
magnificent and radiant Resurrection.
You broke the bonds of death and rose from the
grave as a Conqueror.
You reconciled heaven and earth.
Our life had no hope of eternal happiness before You
redeemed us.
Your Resurrection has washed away our sins, restored
our innocence and brought us joy.
How inestimable is the tenderness of Your Love![113]
Amen.

The prayer of St Augustine:

Merciful, holy and faithful Lord Jesus Christ,
you died for our sins and were raised for our justification,
in view of your resurrection,

---

112.   Acts 2:27,31.
113.   www.catholicculture.org/culture/liturgicalyear/prayers/view.cfm?id=1245
        (accessed 17.1.24).

we ask that you would awaken us also from the grave
of our sins and iniquities,
and grant us your grace that we may partake in your
resurrection
at the final resurrection of all the dead.[114]
Amen.

In his ministry, St Patrick was recorded to have seen: 'Thirty and three dead men, some of whom had been many years buried, did this great reviver raise from the dead.'[115] Here are excerpts from one of St Patrick's pertinent priestly prayers:

...I arise today
Through the strength of Christ's birth and His baptism,
Through the strength of His crucifixion and His burial,
Through the strength of His resurrection and His
ascension,
Through the strength of His descent for the judgment
of doom...

I arise today
Through the strength of heaven;
Light of the sun,
Splendour of fire,
Speed of lightning,
Swiftness of the wind,
Depth of the sea,
Stability of the earth,
Firmness of the rock.

114. https://thinkaboutsuchthings.com/easter-prayers/ (accessed 25.1.24).
115. Fr Albert J. Hebert, excerpt from *Saints Who Raised the Dead: True Stories of 400 Resurrection Miracles (Charlotte, NC: TAN Books, 1986)*, https://catholicism.org/saint-patrick-raised-33-people-from-the-dead-here-are-a-few-examples.html (accessed 25.1.24).

I arise today
Through God's strength to pilot me;
God's might to uphold me,
God's wisdom to guide me,
God's eye to look before me,
God's ear to hear me,
God's word to speak for me,
God's hand to guard me,
God's way to lie before me,
God's shield to protect me,
God's hosts to save me
From snares of the devil,
From temptations of vices,
From everyone who desires me ill,
Afar and anear,
Alone or in a multitude.

…Christ with me, Christ before me, Christ behind me,
Christ in me, Christ beneath me, Christ above me,
Christ on my right, Christ on my left,
Christ when I lie down, Christ when I sit down,
Christ in the heart of every man who thinks of me,
Christ in the mouth of every man who speaks of me,
Christ in the eye that sees me,
Christ in the ear that hears me…

I arise today
Through a mighty strength,
the invocation of the Trinity,
Through a belief in the Threeness,
Through a confession of the Oneness

Of the Creator of creation.[116]
Amen.

During a prayer time with the Lord, I was shown another prayer to include in these pages. In the book of Isaiah, we hear about Hezekiah who becomes desperately sick. The prophet declares: 'you will die' (2 Kings 20:1). Hezekiah, then cries out to live, pleading with the Lord God. The Lord then sees the bitter cries and tears of the king and gives him fifteen more years of peace and deliverance during his reign. This is a part Hezekiah's prayer and song found in Isaiah 38:10 from the Tree of Life Bible, which can be used to cry out to the Lord God in time of need for yourself or others. The best prayers come directly from the Word of God, which can be applied to our own situations. We can cry out to the Lord in heartfelt prayer. This is Hezekiah's song and prayer:

I said: 'In the prime of my life,
I am to enter the gates of Sheol.[117]
I am deprived of the rest of my years.'
I said: 'I will not see ADONAI,
ADONAI, in the land of the living.
I will look on humanity no longer
among the inhabitants of the world.
Like a shepherd's tent,
my dwelling is pulled up and carried away from me.
Like a weaver I rolled up my life.
He cuts me off from the loom.

---

116. www.journeywithjesus.net/poemsandprayers/668-saint-patrick-prayer (accessed 30.1.24).
117. Sheol is the place of the dead; there seem to be different areas in 'hell' (gnashing of teeth, pit, hellfire) as in heaven (throne room, court room, glass sea).

From day until night You make my end.
I stilled my soul till morning.

Like a lion, He will break all my bones.
From day till night You make my end.
Like a swallow or a crane, I whisper,
I moan like a dove.
My eyes are weary, looking upward.
ADONAI, I am oppressed, be my security!
What should I say?
For He has spoken to me –
He Himself has done it!
I will wander about all my years
because of the bitterness of my soul.
ADONAI, by such things men live,
and my spirit has life in them too.
Restore me to health,
and let me live!
Behold, it was for my own shalom
that I had great bitterness.
You have loved my soul
out of the Pit of destruction!
For You have flung all my sins
behind Your back.
For Sheol cannot thank You,
death cannot praise You.
Those who go down to the Pit
cannot hope for Your faithfulness.
The living, the living – they praise You –
as I do today.
A father makes Your faithfulness
known to his children.
ADONAI will save me.

So we will play my songs on stringed instruments
all the days of our life in the House of ADONAI.'[118]
Amen.

Hezekiah has faith, even in his bitterness, on his deathbed, that the Lord would heal him even in his weakness and illness. Let us reach out and commune with the Lord; He wants to know our hearts and wants us all to 'choose life' (Deuteronomy 30:19). Hezekiah was given fifteen more years of life on earth before he passed away, to be with his Lord. Cry out to the Lord, even in your pain. The Lord loves you and has sent Jesus, His beloved Son, to save, heal and set you free. You can be raised up from your sick bed. Commune with the Lord of your life and cry out to Him!

Resurrection testimony

Our pastor at Living Word Church, Fareham, has set up a school of prayer in recent years, which has been a great encouragement to many, to pray 'the hours' throughout the day, in keeping with the model of Jesus and the early Church. He has his own resurrection testimonies to relate. As a church and family, we had prayed him back from death's door in 2022. The following is Christopher Wickland's testimony from death to life written from his wife, Tracey Wickland's perspective when he died in 2019:

On Friday 29 November 2019, it was Chris' day off. I stayed at home to tidy up after the kitchen building work havoc, and Chris planned to take the children to a local theme park. When they arrived, they found

---

118. Isaiah 38:10–20, TLV.

the park closed. Apparently, there was some debate between the cinema and a trampolining centre. The trampolining won! Our daughter, age eleven, tells me while trampolining Chris felt a bit funny and sat on the side. He told her he felt sick and dizzy and was breathing heavily. She thought he fell asleep briefly and she woke him. He then told her their session was nearly over and he was going to get their stuff from the locker room. She saw him walk through and lie down on his back on a bench in the locker room and be sick. Chris had had a Sudden Cardiac Arrest (SCA).

There was a member of the public standing next to him who was first-aid trained and immediately realised something was wrong. She shouted for the staff who got Chris on his side and started CPR. They also had a defibrillator on site which they used to give him four shocks before his heart began to beat again. An ambulance was on its way. The theme park covers a big area with many pathways. If it had happened on a ride or between rides, it's more than likely no one would have got to Chris quickly enough. If they had decided on the cinema, the children could have thought he was sleeping in the dark. By being at the trampolining centre that day, he had instant access to CRP and the defibrillator. Most SCA – more than 90 per cent – result in death, as no one is around with CPR and a defibrillator. God put Chris in the right place at the right time that day; somewhere he should not really have been or had planned to be. Worse still, it could have happened a little later with Chris in the car with the children on the motorway.

The ambulance arrived quickly and took him to Southampton General Hospital, the heart hospital of the South. Again, God speedily delivered Chris to exactly the right place. There was no delay, as there often can be, I'm told, transferring him to Intensive Care. Chris was put into an induced coma for several days. His heart was beating on its own. He had assisted breathing and many IVs, monitors, and assistance to keep him stable and cool.

The staff of the NHS were absolutely amazing. Christians from many different churches and parts of the world began to pray; they held prayer meetings, they prayed in their small groups; they prayed in their churches, and they prayed throughout the day and night. I prayed as I sat with him, and read Scripture over Chris right from when I first got to him in A&E. Friends sat and prayed over him in the night when I needed sleep. Even people Chris had offended over the years put aside differences and prayed fervently for him. I don't think the enemy quite knew what he was starting as the church rallied and rose up.

On the Saturday we had a family meeting with the doctor. It was very bleak. We were told Chris had had fourteen minutes down time (no heartbeat), but that he was fit and young. He was most likely to not die. However, he had had some negative neurological responses and there was likely to be some brain damage and the next days would be an assessment of how much. As they began to remove sedation, they warned that Chris might not wake at all, or he might wake with varying degrees of brain damage. I was told the encephalitis Chris had had years before would be a walk in the park in comparison to the options before us. Worst case scenario, if he did wake, we would see him in a nursing home.

Resurrection Prayers

I was told I couldn't be there as they reduced the sedation, in case they needed to give him emergency treatment. As I sat beside him on Saturday night, his body was yellow and black, blue and swollen. Nothing looked good. I picked up the Gideons International hospital Bible and it opened at to Hebrews 11:1: 'To have faith is being sure of what we hope for and certain of what we do not see'. I needed to take my eyes off of what was right in front of me. On Sunday morning, as churches across the country were praying for Chris, the hospital began to lift the sedation. I was with him despite being told earlier I could not be. I read Psalm 91, Romans 8:11 and the hymn: 'Rise Up, O Men of God!'[119] over him as he began to move. It was a slow process over several hours and he looked truly awful as he opened his eyes, and they rolled as he writhed on the bed.

As the doctors gathered to test him, I felt a bit embarrassed about praying and reading over him, but one of the doctors was a lapsed Christian and told me to keep reading! Over the course of the day Chris began to respond to the tests. He opened his eyes, he wriggled his toes, he poked his tongue out. Several hours later they removed the breathing tube, and later, he spoke. I stayed with him that night as he asked questions.

Over the next few days, he asked the same questions over and over and I began to worry for his short-term memory. I asked the Christians to pray again. Less than 10 per cent of SCAs return to normal. Today is Day Eleven following his SCA. You wouldn't

119. https://hymnary.org/text/rise_up_o_men_of_god (accessed 17.1.24).

know. He has a clear and sound mind. As yet, they can find nothing wrong with his body. They will (most likely), fit him with an ICD (a super-clever, on board, little defibrillator). God is good and faithful! If Chris had died for good, then God would still be good and faithful, but He chose to return him to us and I'm beyond thankful.[120]

Our pastor has had a few brushes with death and am pleased to say, God has given him more years of flourishing life.

Final testimony

The final testimony of this book is the most recent. It is from one of my good friend's fathers-in-law and was given in an interview.

My friend's dad collapsed one night in the middle of July 2022. He woke up and was feeling strange so got up and tried to switch on the light. As he did so, he collapsed, waking his wife.

He remembers his leg feeling heavy, a strange sensation creeping across his face and finding it very difficult to breathe. His wife immediately tried to call the ambulance to take her husband to their nearest hospital, to be told that no ambulances were available. Distraught, she called time and again and given the same answer while he was gasping for breath. Eventually their two sons, came to the rescue,

---

120.   Tracey Wickland, pastor, Living Word Church Network testimony. Edited for the purposes of this book.

bringing a van to take their father to Hospital. The father only remembers feeling the pain in his leg and thinking that he was having a mild stroke. He lost consciousness in the hospital, and after this, they gave him the tests he needed, such as an MRI and a test to check where there were any blood clots. His wife and her two sons were with him and at this point his wife took over the story: 'We were praying and crying continually during our hospital visits, keeping close to our dear one.'

The doctors prepared the family, indicating that the patient would not live, even as they sent him in an ambulance to another specialist hospital to Liverpool. All the while the wife and her sons prayed and asked others to pray for their dad. Again, they were told, on arriving at Liverpool, that the chances of their loved one making it were very slim and to prepare for the worst. The hospital asked what sort of lifestyle he had led: Did he drink? Smoke? Exercise? His wife said no to all vices and, yes, he took a walk most days. They mentioned that his survival odds were extremely slim. There was a team of five consultants looking after this dear man, who had so many clots in his heart, leg and brain.

The patient was in the hospital for four weeks. His wife and her sons hired a house nearby and set up a prayer and visiting vigil for their loved one. They prayed and visited every day, praying morning, noon and night and asking others to pray. During this time, one of the blood clots buried itself in one of the holes in the man's heart, which was a tiny miracle, and was good news as it stopped the bleeding; thereafter the man's body began healing.

The couple attribute their faith in God and prayer to his miraculous recovery and the fact that he also did not need to have any heart surgery whatsoever. The doctors mentioned that he was one in tens of thousands of people to survive such an attack. Some medics called him a 'walking miracle'.

I asked the man and his wife, who at the time of this interview were at home, with him healing and becoming stronger and stronger by the day. I asked them– what would they say to people who needed to know keys about living a resurrection lifestyle? They told me seven things to remember:

1. God is an awesome God.
2. Focus on the life, death and resurrection of Jesus.
3. Thank God every day of your life and for life itself.
4. God is there all the time for you.
5. Pray to God for anything and everything, especially salvation for loved ones.
6. Give your wrongs to God.
7. Trust in the Lord, as the Lord's love endures forever![121]

Final prayer

I would love to encourage you in your faith that the Spirit of the Most High is at work on earth and in you and I. On reading Psalm 104, a beautiful sentence was highlighted to me about the incredible God we serve:

121. Testimony given over WhatsApp on 30 August 2023. Written by author with permission. Edited for the purposes of this book.

You send forth Your Spirit; they are created and You renew the face of the earth.

(v. 30)

From meditating on this verse, I had a sense that God's Spirit enables creative miracles on earth, which we are made from, and renews all who seek Him first, His kingdom and His righteousness,[122] peace and joy in the Holy Spirit.

Dear Lord, Most High,
We thank You for renewing us today.
We thank You for Your creative resurrection love, power and the sound mind of Messiah in us.
Transform our minds to be more like Yours this day.
Create in us a clean heart and renew a right spirit within each of us.[123]
Do a creative work of healing in our bodies as needed, Lord, Holy Spirit.
Do a creative work of peace in our minds and souls; free us from all evil, Lord.
It is in your strength that we arise as Your betrothed;
We can go out and do Your work of lovingkindness,
Due to your tender mercies.
Do these things that we may bring glory to You,
To Your great name, Jesus,
our beautiful Saviour and Lord.
Amen.

---

122. Matthew 6:33.
123. Based on Psalm 51:10, ESV.